SALES
yoga

A Transformational Practice
For
Opening Doors and Closing Deals

Scott Wintrip

"I've worked with many thought leaders across the globe in my role as CEO of the largest global coaching training institution and I've yet to see such an innovative approach to selling. This book should be on the desk of every sales leader and in the hands of every salesperson out there."

– Sandy Vilas, MCC, CEO, CoachInc.com

"Having written 6 books and worked with hundreds of authors, I know *Sales Yoga* will be a game-changer for everyone who reads it and implements the ideas. Scott Wintrip's approach is insightful and one-of-a-kind."

– Sam Horn, Intrigue Expert and author of POP!

Scott nails the current reality in selling—buyers want to buy but they don't want to be sold to. This book is very thought provoking and compelling for any sales professional, giving you valuable insight and strategies on how to get buyers to sell themselves, and makes selling much easier and beneficial to everyone involved. The current quotes also make this book fun and provocative.

– Jim Pickett, Certified Sales Professional, Computer Manufacturing/
IT Industry

Sales Yoga is packed with tangible take-always and action-able ideas. Our global sales team has implemented many of these practical concepts and they are having a very positive impact on our ability to bring in new business while expanding existing relationships.

– Andrea Hopkey, President, Technical Services Firm

When it comes to innovative sales ideas, Scott Wintrip is the leading thought leader you must pay attention to. Read *Sales Yoga*, apply the concepts and you will transform your sales success.

– Chad Barr, President, CB Software Systems and author of Million
Dollar Web Presence

What a page-turner! The short chapters make *Sales Yoga* an easy read. The combination of compelling ideas, interesting stories, and intriguing quotes got me thinking and acting differently.
— *Andrew Meyer, Personal Banker, Major US Financial Institution*

Sales Yoga

Author's Note and Acknowledgments   vii

Foreword   ix

Introduction   xiii

Section One: So, What is *Sales Yoga*?

1. *Sales Yoga* Is A Way of Life and a Way of Business   3

Section Two: What is the Step-by-Step S.A.L.E.S. Y.O.G.A. Process?

2. S = Start *HalfTalking*   13
3. A = Adopt a "Do-Over" Mentality   23
4. L = Launch, Lead, or Lock?   31
5. E = Emphasize Value, Not Price   39
6. S = Shields Up or Shields Down?   47
7. Y = Yet   59
8. O = Objections Are Opportunities   67

9. G = Go It Together   77
10. A = Appreciate and Celebrate   87

Section Three: What Other *Sales Yoga* Principles Can I Integrate into My Practice?

11. Keep Your Totems Top of Mind   97
12. Manage Your Moods With Mantras   105
13. Sell with Integrity   111
14. Give Your Brain and Your Buyer Homework   117
15. Remember that Practice Makes Profit   125
16. Strive For Excellence, Not Perfection   133
17. Shape Your Sales Behavior; Don't Shame It   141
18. Be Clear That Money is a Priority, Not a Resource   147
19. Sell The Front of the Box, Not the Features   153
20. Provocative *Launching Questions* Pay Off   159
21. Persist … Gently   167
22. Do This When a Client Says, "I'm Sorry, There's
    Someone Else"   175
23. Fire Clients Who Are Not a Match   183
24. Always Be Collaborating   191
25. Don't Try to Force A Downward Dog   199
26. The Power of Referrals   207

Section Four: Action Plan and Summary

27. What's Next? Create Your Sales Yogi Destiny   217

About the Author   223

Want to Work With Scott Wintrip?   227

Author's Note

It is important to me to honor the confidentiality of my clients. Please know that all of the stories and examples in this book are true and pulled from my real-life experiences…however I've changed some of the identifying details so my clients and audience members can trust their privacy is being protected.

Dedication

To my son, Benjamin. Thank you for teaching me the true value of inquiry. Yes, that means I even appreciate the thousands of times you asked me, "Why?"

Acknowledgments

"When you drink the water; remember the well."
– Chinese proverb

Thank you to my customers who bought what I sold and also to the prospects who told me, "No." My experiences with each of you have made me the Sales Yogi I am today.

Special thanks to my bonus daughter Mackenzie for reminding me not to take myself too seriously. And to my wife and best friend, Holly: your encouragement has been life changing.

Foreword

To Sell or Not to Sell...Is Not A Question

Peter Drucker, the inventor of corporate strategy, famously pointed out that the first job of any business is to have a customer. Without successful sales, we have no customers—and no business. That's why there are thousands of books on the sales process.

It's the same reason there are so many books on medical practices and procedures. We're talking lifeblood.

But these books, whether on medicine or sales, overwhelmingly look at traditional approaches. It wasn't until recently, incredibly enough, that doctors admitted to the need to wash their hands continually throughout their day. Even today, hospital deaths are often caused by illness introduced to the patient while in the hospital!

Sales books are still pontificating about features and benefits or, worse, "finding the pain." The pain I've found is usually in trying to adapt such dated advice to selling in the 21st Century.

I've consulted with nearly 200 Fortune 1000 companies, written 42 books, traveled to 60 countries, and coached a couple of thousand executives and entrepreneurs. My frame of reference isn't shabby. I've found that for anyone who sells—and honestly, who doesn't?—it's time for some alternative medicine.

That's what Scott Wintrip has provided in *Sales Yoga.*

Scott takes you through a different regimen, one oriented toward acquiring business in modern times, despite the volatility in the economy, technology, social mores, and demographics. He reinvigorates you with a new energy and purpose. He'll help you to stretch—your mind.

As Scott points out, "Flogging is not a yoga pose." So stop beating yourself up and start beating others to the sale.

- Alan Weiss, PhD
- Author, Million Dollar Referrals and Alan Weiss on Consulting
among 50 other books.

Introduction

*"It's easy to make a buck.
It's tougher to make a difference."*

– Tom Brokaw

Are you frustrated with the negative stereotypes—i.e., pushy, smarmy, manipulative—directed at salespeople? Me too.

Wouldn't it be wonderful if you could make a buck *and* a positive difference for everyone you dealt with while being highly respected at the same time?

You can! It's called *Sales Yoga.*

Sales Yoga is a collaborative (vs. coercive) approach to sales where the needs of *all* parties are met. It's a mutually rewarding process in which everyone involved prospers.

The Genesis of *Sales* Yoga?

"The only danger is not to evolve."
– Jeff Bezos, founder of Amazon

Are you wondering how *Sales Yoga* got started?

I'll give the whole story about its origin in Chapter 1. For now, suffice it to say the old-fashioned, domineering, "get a deal at any cost" sales approach used to be my SOP (Standard Operating Procedure).

I was making a lot of money, but I was also unhealthy and unhappy, and my perpetual bad mood was affecting my family, friends and work relationships.

The way I was taught to do sales—the classic "Always Be Closing" mentality from the infamous movie *Glenngarry Glen Ross* with Jack Lemmon, Alec Baldwin, etc.—was taking a serious toll on me and everyone around me.

Then, I discovered yoga. Believe me, I was as surprised as anyone. I used to think of yoga as a non-athletic, kind of "airy-fairy" activity that consisted mostly of sitting on a mat and doing some mild stretches.

Wrong.

In fact, 20 minutes into my first class, I discovered yoga was one of the most physically challenging and emotionally rewarding activities I'd ever tried.

Over the next few months, I also discovered renewed energy, a more positive outlook, and a peacefulness that positively permeated all aspects of my life. And yes, that included my approach to sales.

I started integrating my epiphanies gleaned from yoga into my work...and clients noticed.

Program participants told me they appreciated this fresh approach that combined "best practice" sales techniques with the centeredness that comes from practicing yoga. Consulting and advising clients told me my innovative approaches were helping them achieve even more satisfying success at work, at home and in their community.

My friends also noticed I had changed and asked, "What happened?!"

When I told them about the amazing transformation yoga had set into motion, they told me, "You should write a book about this. People could benefit from what you've learned. You have an opportunity—and a responsibility—to share this with others."

So, here it is. My offering to you.

In this book, I share how to integrate *Sales Yoga* into your professional and personal interactions, and how evolutionary it can be to approach all your relationships with the goal of collaborating vs. coercing.

Please note: I'm not claiming to be an expert who knows everything there is to know about yoga. It takes a lifetime to master all of yoga's depth, complexity and potential.

My goal is simply to offer a methodology I've developed that has already benefited thousands of salespeople across the globe.

I hope you too will discover the many rewards of integrating the timeless principles of yoga into your on-the-job and off-the-job interactions. Choosing to use these *Sales Yoga* techniques can bring much-welcomed abundance and well-being into your life and to the lives of the people you touch.

Who Will This Book Help?

"To become what we are capable of becoming is the only end of life." – Robert Louis Stevenson

Do you want to:

- Create cooperative relationships with people where everyone wins?
- Learn more compassionate ways of genuinely connecting with people?

- Sell your ideas, products and services ethically and effectively?
- Meet and exceed your sales quotas while meeting the true needs of clients?
- Deepen your pool of prospects through conscious listening of what they want most?
- Discover how to be present instead of feeling rushed, distracted, anxious?
- Transform stress and anger into a peacefulness that permeates your life?
- Stretch your communication skills so you're more confident when selling?
- Earn a *good* living by adding value for everyone you meet?

If you answered yes to any of the above questions, you're in the right place.

You don't even have to be a salesperson to benefit from this book. Face it; we're all in sales. Anytime we have an idea, product, service or request that we want supported, approved, bought or recommended—that involves selling.

You can use these *Sales Yoga* approaches in the workplace to close a multi-million dollar deal *and* at home to motivate your teen to do his homework (I've used *Sales Yoga* to do both). You can use them with current *and* prospective customers. You can even use them with co-workers and employees. You'll discover everyone benefits when you use these techniques because they create mutually beneficial results for all involved.

Want to increase the tangible impact this book has on you and your sales team?

Buy a copy of *Sales Yoga* for every one of your employees, and announce to your staff that you'll be working your way through the book...together.

Ask everyone to read the assigned chapter and to be ready to discuss it at the next meeting. I've deliberately kept the chapters short, five to eight pages, so even your busiest salesperson can find time to read it over the course of a week.

You can create even more impact, and develop the leadership skills of your team members, by asking a different employee each week to facilitate a ten-minute discussion on "their" chapter. For example, Serena has Chapter 1 for March 3rd. Jorge has Chapter 2 for March 10th. Taylor has Chapter 3 for March 17th, etc.

Encourage the person in charge to be creative. Give them the autonomy to conduct their chapter discussion any way they feel will be most beneficial for the group.

Rotating the chair of your *Sales Yoga* discussion groups gives your meetings a welcome variety. Everyone looks forward to them because they know it will be different instead of same-old, same-old. It may even set up a friendly competition in which meeting chairs try to "out-do" each other to have the most interesting, useful discussion. Plus, this gives team members an opportunity to be in charge, develop their speaking skills and the ability to run a productive meeting that benefits all involved.

Ready to discover how to take care of buyers from the very beginning so they trust you, do repeat business with you and voluntarily recommend you to others? Ready to learn how to create mutually rewarding relationships in which everyone wins?

If so, turn the page and let's go.

Section One:

So, What is *Sales Yoga?*

"Are you doing what you're doing today because it works, or because it's what you were doing yesterday?"

– Dr. Phil McGraw

Chapter 1:
Sales Yoga is a Way of Life and a Way of Business

*"Yoga is almost like music in a way;
there's no end to it."*

– Sting

What is *Sales Yoga*?

Why is it worth considering?

If your current sales approach is getting good results, why is it worth trying?

Sales Yoga is a "collaborative approach to meeting the shared needs of a buyer and seller."

When done right, the buyer gets what s/he needs (i.e., a product, service or something of value) and the seller gets what s/he needs (i.e., compensation, an account or something of value). When done right, *Sales Yoga* creates an equitable quid pro quo.

How is this done?

Instead of using an old-fashioned sales model of focusing solely on how to get what WE want—we focus on creating an outcome and relationship that serves BOTH of us. Even salespeople who believe they are focusing on the customer are often still perceived as only being in it for themselves.

The means to creating this type of mutually rewarding relationship comes from using the timeless principles and practices of yoga.

In the coming chapters, you'll learn exactly how to use a variety of *Sales Yoga* poses and practices to stay centered in a mindset that leads to mutually beneficial interactions for all involved. The purpose of this chapter is to share a few more details about my initiation into yoga and how it's lead to a better way of life—and a better way of business—for me and others.

My Introduction to Yoga

"All adventures into new territory are scary."
– Astronaut Sally Ride

I must admit that I approached my first yoga class with some apprehension. I didn't know what to expect. And when we don't know what we're getting into, we're anxious. In fact, anxiety is defined as "not knowing."

I thought yoga would probably involve some sitting, stretching, and deep breathing…maybe even some chanting?

And, that's exactly what happened…for the five minute warm up. The rest of the 55-minute class was one of the most demanding, exhilarating, athletic experiences of my life. I had no idea just how *hard* yoga could be!

After one class, I was hooked. What really "sold" me was the feeling I had walking out of that class. Let me be clear, I hadn't found "Nirvana." I wasn't ready to quit my job, fly to the Himalayas and become a Buddhist monk or anything. I'm not suggesting that yoga is a miracle pill or a quick fix for instant enlightenment.

What I felt was…calm.

For the first time, in as long as I could remember, I didn't feel stress. I wasn't carrying around a teeth-clenched tension, low-grade resentment, or even the racing thoughts about all that I had to accomplish.

I walked out of that yoga studio with a sense of hope and renewal. After a few more classes, and some serious self-reflection, the pieces began to fall in to place.

Once again, I'm not saying I could instantly, effortlessly do Tree Pose and stand in perfect balance on one leg. My mind kept having a mind of its own, and I was still hopping and bobbling all over the place. But I was already reaping benefits.

Benefits such as weight loss without even trying. I hadn't changed my diet but the pounds and inches started dropping off.

Benefits such as increased energy and clarity. I was a happier, more centered, human being. I hadn't anticipated that the answer to my growing dissatisfaction with the sales profession was in that yoga studio with all those moms, students, retirees and executives...but there it was.

I remember driving home one morning from class and realizing, "If I can practice sales like I practice yoga, everything will get better." And that's exactly what happened.

You may be thinking, "Sounds too good to be true. Plus, I've got a family to feed, bills to pay, quotas to meet. I can't afford to experiment with something if it's not guaranteed to pay off. There's no way I can jeopardize my livelihood."

I hear you. To be honest, I had some initial concerns that a more compassionate yoga-like approach to business might end up with ME being happier and with customers liking me more... but I would be losing accounts to more aggressive, less scrupulous salespeople who were pressuring clients and relentlessly chasing down deals.

Didn't happen. My worries were unnecessary.

In fact, as I began to integrate *Sales Yoga* techniques, my work relationships *and* results improved. I experienced a substantial increase in income *and* in customer loyalty. I started looking forward to work instead of dreading it. New buyers that normally would have run the opposite direction as soon as they spotted me were suddenly willing to sit down and have a genuine conversation.

What's the Business Case for Sales Yoga?

"Money doesn't make you happy; but happiness makes you money." – rap mogul Russell Simmons

What do Dr. Dean Ornish, Groupon CEO Andrew Mason, Russell Simmons and former Supreme Court Justice Sandra Day O'Connor have in common?

They're all respected executives, entrepreneurs and leaders who believe their yoga practice has contributed to their business success.

Susan Payton, President of *Egg Marketing & Communications*, wrote an insightful article for *Small Business Trends* entitled *10 Things Yoga Teaches Us About Small Business Ownership* Two of the many yoga-mentality benefits that show up in the workplace include:

1. **You'll never be perfect.** Your industry, technology, marketing techniques and competitors continue to evolve—so should you.
2. **Getting out of your comfort zone is a good thing.** Instead of sticking to poses you're comfortable with because they're easy, yoginis stretch themselves.

A *TIME* magazine article entitled *The Power of Yoga* says, "Stars do it. Athletes do it. Judges in the highest courts do it. Millions of Americans include some form of yoga in their fitness regimen. They rush from their high-pressure jobs to tune in to the authoritatively mellow voice of an instructor, gently urging them to solder a 'union' (the literal translation of the Sanskrit word "yoga") between mind and body."

Just how many people practice yoga?

A 2012 study by *Yoga Journal* reported, "20.4 million Americans practice yoga, up from 15.8 million in 2008. And they spend $2 billion on yoga retreats."

And as I discovered, yoga isn't just for those into Eastern religions, meditation or alternative health practices. As Bjorn Hanson, Dean of Hospitality, Tourism and Sports Management at NYU, says, "Yoga cuts across all age groups and demographics; it's universal. That's why many hotels and airports are installing yoga rooms and classes for busy, exhausted, stressed-out professionals who travel."

The popular *WebMD* website lists dozens of health benefits of yoga including "increased core strength, endurance and flexibility." Plus it says, "Nearly every yoga student reports they feel 'happier and more contented' after class."

What's this mean for you? As you're about to discover, the techniques in this book can not only help you build a better union between your mind and body; they can help you build a better union between you and your customers and co-workers.

Are you ready to jump into the actual techniques that can help you do all the above? If so, review the Action Plan on the next page and then prepare yourself to learn the nine-step S.A.L.E.S. Y.O.G.A process.

Action Plan for Chapter 1

"Be at least as interested in what goes on inside you as what happens outside.   If you get the inside right, the outside will fall into place."
– Eckhart Tolle, The Power of Now

As Eckhart Tolle says, if you get the inside of you right, the outside of you will also feel right, and all your relationships will benefit as a result. Take a moment to ask yourself these questions and reflect on your answers. Your responses will serve as a foundation for your commitment to do what it takes to become a Sales Yogi.

---

1. Am I tired of all the negative stereotypes associated with salespeople?
2. Do I want to be proud of being a salesperson? Of the sales profession as a whole?
3. Was I taught to "always be closing?" Has that "hard-sell" mentality taken a toll on me and the people I deal with at work and at home? How so?
4. Have I tried yoga before or am I already a yoga practitioner and enthusiast? If so, what benefits have I already experienced from yoga?
5. Am I open to new sales approaches that would benefit me and my customers? Do I have any doubts or fears that would hold me back? If so, what are they?
6. How would it feel to tell people I work in sales, and have each and every one of them respect that instead of making a face or a sarcastic joke at my expense?
7. Do I have a Sales Yogi avatar? A thought leader who is a role model of someone who integrates the principles of yoga into business? Who is that?

Section 2:

What is the Step-by-Step

S.A.L.E.S. Y.O.G.A. Process?

*"To do what you love
and feel that it matters;
how could anything be more fun?"*

– Katharine Graham, Washington Post

Chapter 2:
S = Start *HalfTalking*

"For most people; the opposite of talking isn't listening; it's waiting."

– Fran Liebowitz

Do you know salespeople like this; they don't really listen; they just wait for their turn to talk? Not much fun, is it?

As discussed in the introduction, many salespeople are factory-default set to "talk." If you've been to the same types of trainings I have, even if the program description mentions listening, the vast majority of techniques still focus on *what* to say, *how* to say it, *when* to say it and to *only* say it to decision makers who can give you a contract.

I was on vacation in California about ten years ago and ventured out to a comedy club for some late-night entertainment. Not long after I settled at my table, the house lights went down and the MC stepped out onto the stage.

"Ladies and gentleman, thank you for joining us tonight. Let me be the first to give you the good news…tonight is *not* amateur night."

Nice way to open. I chuckled with the rest of the crowd and relaxed into my chair. Okay, not-amateur night, let me have it.

"Our first guy is 26-year-old Nathan from No One Cares, Indiana. Nathan, come on out and make the crowd happy or you're washing dishes to pay for that beer you're drinking."

Ouch! Nathan walks out with a good-natured smile and proceeds to unleash his repertoire. I have to admit, by the fourth joke; I was beginning to think the MC had lied about it not being amateur night. Then, Nathan rolls out this provocative one-liner:

"Alright folks, tell me this. How does a deaf guy spot a salesman? He's the only one whose lips never stop moving."

Really?!?

I don't know whether it was because it was politically incorrect or just not funny, but no one in the crowd laughed.

But what caught my attention was this: Every person in the room gave a knowing smirk and nodded their head in agreement.

I was kind of annoyed initially because, once again, salespeople were the butt of a joke; but I realized that Nathan had made a solid point.

People often think of a sales pitch purely in the context of being verbally assaulted or imprisoned. They see us coming and rather than wondering if we have anything of value to offer; they head the other direction. How can we change that?

Practice *Mind Over Mouth*

"I never learn anything talking. I only learn things when I ask questions and listen." – Lou Holtz

Lou Holtz made his career as an acclaimed football coach. He was even inducted into the College Football Hall of Fame in 2008.

Now, the stereotype of a coach is that he's the guy on the field yelling orders, calling plays, running the show and telling people what to do.

Yet, here is Holtz, cautioning us to learn through listening. Wise advice.

Rebecca, a consulting client of mine in 2003, worked as a sales representative in the fashion industry. Her buyers were typically mid-to-high end boutiques and department stores where she specialized in popular clothing and accessories geared toward "tweens", teens and 20-somethings.

Rebecca was well aware of the ever-changing tastes of her target customers and worked with me to hone her skills to capture and keep the attention of her buyers.

During our initial consultation, Rebecca laid out her goals. "Scott, you've got it, I've got it. In our industry we've all got it: the gift for gab. I know I can talk, I know I can sell. The problem is, it takes me way too long to get across what I want to say. I can hear myself yakking and I'm thinking, 'Rebecca, shut up! You're babbling and they're getting bored,' but I can't seem to help myself. I know I need to listen more but my mouth gets the best of me."

I complimented Rebecca on her self-awareness. "Good for you. Most salespeople don't even realize how much they talk. They go on and on and never see the glazed eyes or yawning. I've even seen salespeople continue their pitch *after* the client has pulled out their phone and started checking emails. What I really think is they're playing *Angry Birds*."

I told Rebecca, "You're on the right track by admitting to the habit many of us have, "Our mouth runs the show and our buyers just wish they could go."

Rebecca told me, "Here's the problem. I know I have the habit, I just don't seem to have the willpower to change it. I try to stop talking, I mean, I really try, but I always end up just chattering away. How do I get a grip on this?"

Again, I validated Rebecca's honest self-assessment. I told her, "You're right, it takes dedication to change a habit. Change can be anxiety-provoking and when we get anxious, we often default back to our most *practiced* behavior, not our new behavior."

I told Rebecca, "Here's what we're going to do. We're going to play a game called *Mind Over Mouth*. But first, tell me this. If you were going to reward yourself for a job well done, for successfully changing a habit, how would you do it?"

Rebecca took a moment and then lit up: "Shoes!" she said. "I love shoes. It's not an addiction or *anything*. I don't have a billion pairs of shoes in my closet, but when I want to reward myself, a pair of brand new shoes makes me feel really good."

"Shoes it is."

From there on, Rebecca and I set up the *Mind Over Mouth* game.

Make *Mind Over Mouth* Measurable with *HalfTalk*

*"You know what we need? A 12-step group for
non-stop talkers. We're going to call it 'On and On Anon."
– comedian Paula Poundstone*

I told her, "You've heard the saying, 'We can't manage it if we don't measure it?'"

"Sure," she said.

"Well, it's easier to change long-time habits when we give ourselves *measurable* goals. So your goal is to *decrease your talking by 50%*. For example, if you normally talk 80% of the time, your target is to cut that down to 40%. Your goal is to always make sure your client does MUCH MORE talking than you do.

"There's an easy way to keep track of this. At the end of every conversation, just ask yourself, *'Who did the most talking?'*

"If it's YOU…that's not *HalfTalk*. Any time you did more talking than the other person that means you did more speaking than listening … and that's not *Sales Yoga*."

Rebecca said, "You're right, *HalfTalk* gives me a metric to hold myself accountable for drawing them out instead of me non-stop talking. But what about the shoes? Where do they come in?"

"You're going to keep a sales journal. At the end of each meeting with a client, ask yourself, 'Who did the most talking?' If it was the CLIENT, you get 100 points. When you get 1000 points, the equivalent of 10 successful *HalfTalk* sales conversations, you get a new pair of shoes."

Now, Rebecca was a realistic person. She knew this would probably turn out to be "easier said than done" so she made the commitment to play *Mind Over Mouth* for a minimum of three months. You've probably heard the research that says it takes at least 18 days, usually much longer, to form a new habit, and she wanted to give herself a reasonable amount of time to overcome her default habit of talking, talking, talking.

Rebecca reported her results in our weekly check-in calls. The first week, she was rather embarrassed to admit she only had three *HalfTalk* wins. The second week she was up to 8…and on the third week she started off our call with this:

"Scott, *HalfTalk* works! And *Mind Over Mouth* works too. After our call, I'm on my way to the mall to buy *a* new pair of shoes. And, I can afford them because I picked up *three* new clients this week."

If you have a tendency to talk too much, keeping a sales journal to track your *HalfTalk* successes can help you focus on your positive progress. *Mind Over Mouth* is not about using your "will" to *force* yourself to stop talking so much. It's about using your "want" to *facilitate* yourself to start listening more.

In the long term, we respond better to rewards than recriminations. Praise works better than punishment. By having a tangible way to measure and celebrate her progress, she gave herself incentive to overcome a life-long habit.

Are You Ready to Change the HABIT of Talking Too Much?

"The second half of a man's life is made up of nothing but the accumulation of habits he acquired in the first half."
– Feodor Dostoevsky

For Rebecca, a brand new pair of shoes was sufficient to motivate her to stick with her *HalfTalk* and *Mind over Mouth* goals. How about you? Are your sales habits serving you or sabotaging you? What will it take for you to commit to talk less, listen more? The good news is, you CAN reverse a life-long habit if you have sufficient motivation and if you make your commitment tangible and visible.

These **Seven Steps for Changing Habits** can help. Ask yourself:

---

1. What was a time I successfully changed a habit? Did I stop smoking? Stop showing up late? Stop ordering dessert at restaurants?
2. How did it feel to change a habit that was undermining my health or success?
3. What was the key to my success? What did I do that helped me keep my commitment to myself to turn over a new leaf and do things differently?
4. Did I "go public" with my intentions? Did I ask for help, join a support group, or set up an accountability buddy so I wasn't going it alone?
5. Did I make it tangible and measurable so I could tell when I was progressing and when I was backsliding?

6. How did I motivate myself? What rewards did I promise myself?
7. What specific steps am I going to take to hold myself accountable for *HalfTalk* and *Mind Over Mouth* so I set myself up for success?

This first step of the S.A.L.E.S. Y.O.G.A. process is non-negotiable. Simply stated, *HalfTalk* is the key to making sure we're focused on what the OTHER person wants to say instead of only on what WE want to say. It's the secret to setting up a mutually prosperous interaction. It's a way of putting our clients first... and making sure this is a *two-way* dialogue instead of a *one-way* monologue.

I'll always be grateful to yoga for showing me the benefits of not talking so much. I remember driving home from a yoga class after I'd been doing it for about a month. I felt so calm, so peaceful. I tried to pinpoint what it was, exactly, that contributed to that deeply satisfying sense of centered well-being.

All of a sudden it came to me. For the entire hour of class, I had not said one word. I had listened, I had moved, stretched and balanced with intense concentration; but I did everything in silence.

At that time, silence was contrary to my nature. As mentioned in the Intro, I'm what you might call an "A" personality. I'm driven, intense, and action-oriented. For me to not say anything for an entire hour was the exception to my norm.

And it was nice. I've come to welcome the reverent silence that surrounds me during my yoga sessions. My newfound comfort with quiet has reduced the "get to the point" impatience I used to feel in conversations.

I hope you'll try a yoga class. If you're already a yoga aficionado, you know the peace to be found in mindfulness. If you're new to it, you'll find that talking less, or not talking at all, can help you tune into yourself, your surroundings and what the people around you are feeling, saying, thinking and needing.

And when you do that, your improved "silent sensitivity" will support your commitment to *HalfTalking* and *Mind over Mouth* in your business communications. As a result, you, and everyone you engage with, will benefit.

Action Plan for Chapter 2

"Someone's boring me. I think it's me." – Dylan Thomas

So, how are you going to take action on this first S.A.L.E.S. Y.O.G.A. step to set yourself up for success? How are you going to hold yourself accountable for *HalfTalk* and *Mind Over Mouth?* Are you going to keep a journal, ask a co-worker to "test" you, give yourself a meaningful incentive to make sure you're not boring or offending people with non-stop monologues? Here's an example of Rebecca's *Mind Over Mouth* journal that you can use as a template and adapt for your own purposes:

HalfTalk and *Mind Over Mouth* **Journal**

SMART Goal (Specific, Measurable, Attainable, Rewards, Timeline)	*HalfTalk*: Decrease *my* talking during sales conversation by 50% and clients do MORE than 50% of the talking.
Incentive (What will motivate you?)	Shoes! (Lunch at a favorite restaurant? A massage? Tickets for a concert?)

Points per achieved goal: 100 for each successful *HalfTalk* conversation

Points per reward: 1000 points per pair of shoes

Game Time Frame: 6 Weeks starting March 1st

Target # of Sales Conversations: 60 (with current *and* prospective clients)

Tracking Results: 30 Successful *HalfTalk* conversations
                               30 x 100 points = 3000 points
                               3 points of NEW SHOES

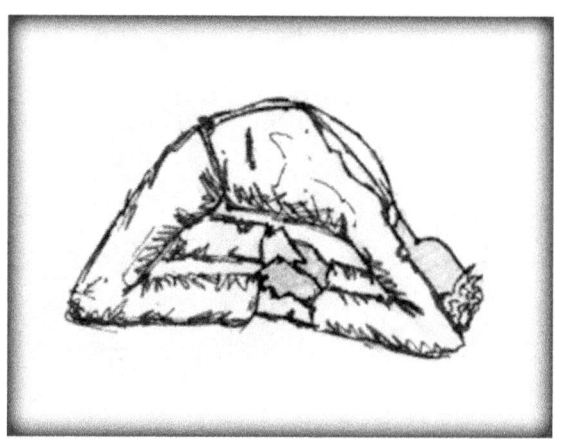

Chapter 3:
A = Adopt a "Do-Over" Mentality

"Use failure as a stepping stone. Don't try to forget mistakes, but don't dwell on them. Don't let them have any of your energy, time, or space."

– Johnny Cash

I was sitting at my dining room table working on a keynote presentation when a commotion from my backyard caught my attention. I walked over to the window to look outside and see what was going on.

My six-year-old son and his BFF (Best Friend Forever) were kneeling on the muddy grass (it'd rained earlier in the day) staring at the ground between them. They both had intense looks of concentration on their muddy faces. I couldn't see what they were doing, but they suddenly startled, looked up at each another, threw their hands up in the air and shouted something with such glee I had to investigate.

I walked outside, but they were so intent on what they were doing, they didn't pay me any attention. They set up some small robot-like contraption on the ground again, leaned back and waited for it to do its thing.

It quickly became clear it wasn't cooperating. It took a few steps and then fell over. Rather than getting frustrated, the two boys looked at each other, simultaneously threw their hands in the air and yelled at the top of their lungs...*"Do Over!"*

They dissolved into giggles and proceeded to do it all over again. I loved their attitude. It was so simple. They were out there, in the mud, failing over and over again. But instead of getting frustrated and giving up, they were having a great time. They seemed to delight in and welcome each "Do-Over" opportunity.

If only we adults were the same way. We can be so hard on ourselves sometimes. If we try something and it doesn't work out the way we hope, instead of delightedly saying "Do-Over," we're more likely to say, "Stupid." Or "What was I thinking?!" or "What a klutz."

Our mental self-talk can be downright vicious. We are often our own worst critics. Failure is often seen as something shameful, something to be regretted.

Fail Forward

"Notice the difference between what happens when a man says to himself, 'I have failed three times,' and what happens when he says, 'I am a failure.'" – S. I. Hayakawa

Children expect failure and are not deterred by it. For them, it is simply part of the learning process. They know that failure is simply an opportunity to begin again...more intelligently this time.

Yogi Berra said, "Man, was that a wrong mistake." They don't call him Yogi for nothing. A key premise of *Sales Yoga* is, *"The only wrong mistake is one we don't learn from."*

We learn absolutely nothing by repeating things we already know. Growth only happens when we get outside our comfort zone and try new things.

Sales Yoga suggests new ways to approach sales. When you try techniques that are different from your norm, they won't work perfectly.

That's when you say "Do-Over." That's when you reflect on what you did that worked—and what you did that didn't. That's when you capitalize on and continue what worked—and you tweak and fine-tune what didn't.

One of my favorite "Do-Over" success stories comes from a speaker colleague who decided she needed to start following up with previous clients. She'd heard, like you probably have, that it's five times easier to get business from a past client than it is to find a new one.

She told me, "I love to speak; I hate to sell. My business has operated successfully on word-of-mouth for years. There's a saying in our industry, 'Your best marketing is your best speech.' Well, that's worked well for me all this time, but the meetings industry has really taken a hit because of the bad economy. So, I went through my files and pulled out the names of 10 of my best clients from the past few years, and starting calling each.

I called the first meeting planner, who is in charge of conventions for a very large association of executives. She took my call, said it was good to hear from me and then asked what I was calling about. I started telling her I wanted to submit a proposal to present at their annual conference. I mentioned my new program and the raves it's received from other groups, and she interrupted me with, "Have you filled out the RFP—Request for Proposals—on our website?"

I told her, "Not yet, I was hoping to talk with you personally and...."

She interrupted me again and said, "Everything you need to do is on that form. Just go ahead and fill that out and submit it and we'll make our decision from that."

I have to admit. I was kind of crushed. I was hoping she'd remember what great evaluations I'd gotten from my previous work with them...but it was clear she didn't even want to talk with me."

Here's where my friend told me, "Scott, before we talked and you told me about your 'Do-Over" philosophy; I would probably have given up in embarrassment and trashed the whole plan to contact previous clients. But I remembered what you said about failure being an opportunity to begin again...more intelligently.

"The next call I was smarter and more sensitive. I started off by saying, 'I know you're busy. May I just have two minutes of your time?' He seemed to appreciate me acknowledging that he had a lot competing for his attention; and after our brief call, he asked me to send my new topic description to him directly as they had a winter meeting coming up he thought this might be perfect for."

Want to know the key to putting mistakes to work *for* you vs. *against* you?

Get rid of the word "should." The word "should," as in "You *should* have emailed first instead of calling out of the blue."

Think about it. The word "should" usually pertains to the past. Do you know anyone who can un-do the past? It is a waste of time to tell yourself—or anyone else—what you *should* have done.

Be a *coach*, not a *critic*. Instead of telling yourself what you did *wrong*; focus on how you can do *it right.*

When you try these new S.A.L.E.S. Y.O.G.A. techniques, they may not work perfectly the first time. That's to be expected. Any new skill takes time to master. Instead of getting upset or impatient with yourself; declare a "Do-Over." Simply focus on how you can do it better next time and turn that mistake into a lesson learned.

My first yoga instructor was a shining example of the difference it can make when we're coached instead of criticized. I was feeling pretty overwhelmed those first few sessions. I couldn't hold my balance for more than a few seconds. My Tree Pose consisted of me hopping around while everyone around me stood tall and held their ground.

Instead of making me feel worse by pointing out everything I was doing wrong, my yoga instructor smiled gently and told me to imagine roots growing down through my feet 10 feet into the ground. Any time I managed to hold the pose a second or two longer, he would nod wisely and encouragingly, helping me stay focused on my improvement and what I could do, instead of what I couldn't.

Be as gentle with yourself as he was with me. Give yourself credit where credit is due so you welcome Do-Over's as an opportunity to do better.

Action Plan for Chapter 3

"Our task is not to fix the blame for the past; it's to fix the course for the future."

– former President John F. Kennedy

Remember, a crucial element of *Sales Yoga* is being willing to stretch ourselves and try new "poses" or approaches.

And when we try new things, we won't do them perfectly. Instead of getting upset and abandoning our efforts with a discouraged "Well, that didn't work," resolve to *fail forward*. Don't *should* on yourself. Figure out what didn't work, fix it and try,

try again. Instead of staying stuck in the status quo, a "Do-Over" mentality will help you grow.

Remember that St. Francis de Sales said, "Have patience with all things, but chiefly have patience with yourself. Do not lose courage in considering your own imperfections, but instantly set about remedying them—every day begin the task anew."

Chapter 4:
L = Launch, Lead or Lock?

"Never stop questioning."

– Albert Einstein

A week after one of my public workshops, I got a call from Cho. He started off with, "I wish I had listened to you."

"Okay," I said, curious about where this was going. "Tell me more."

"I went through the session where you taught the new style of questioning: Launch, Lead or Lock. While I understood it in the moment, I guess I didn't fully integrate it because I fell back on my old habits."

Cho worked for an independently-owned staffing firm in upstate New York. "He told me, "I lost a deal because I used *Leading Questions* when interviewing a potential candidate. You told us that was a no-no, and you were right."

"What happened?" I asked.

"Well, I asked him, 'Are you looking for temporary work or a full-time job?'

"He told me, 'Between those two choices, I would pick temp.'

"I should have paid attention when he said, 'Between those two choices,' but I missed it. I pitched him to my corporate clients and sang his praises, but they weren't interested. Two weeks later, he called me with some bad news. He said, 'I wanted to let you know I got a job through another agency.'

"I'm glad to hear you got a job. I'm curious. How did you find this position?"

He told me one of my competitors had placed him in a temp-to-hire position at a well-known local company with whom I also did business.

I couldn't help myself. I burst out with, "I wish I'd known you were interested in that kind of work. I could have placed you there."

"Yeah," he told me. "Honestly, I made a better connection with you, but you only gave me two choices, temp or full time. I really liked this '3 month try-out' option. If it works out for both of us; it turns into a full-time job. If it doesn't, no harm, no foul."

Cho told me, "That's over $8,000 in commission down the drain. Is there anything I can do to salvage this?"

"Nope," I told him. "It's too late now."

"This sucks. I should have asked him a *Launching Question* like you taught us to. If I'd asked him 'What type of employment arrangement would you prefer?' instead of a *Leading Question* 'Do you want temp or full-time?'…I'd be the one depositing that commission check into my bank account."

Cho is not the only one who makes the mistake of asking *Leading Questions* that unnecessarily limit what unfolds.

The drawback to *Leading Questions* is, when you give people two or three choices, they conclude they only have two or three choices. They pick the one that sounds "best," but there could be other more viable options that haven't even been brought up.

Here are the definitions of three different types of questions:

Launching Questions: They are 10 words or less to ensure they're not confusing, convoluted, or complicated. The brevity of *Launching Questions* helps people to understand them immediately, allowing them to focus more on their answers to these powerful questions. They cannot be answered with a yes or no. They are open-ended so the respondent articulates (sometimes for the first time) what's meaningful to them. They are designed to evoke— pull out—insights as to what's important to the person we're dealing with.

Leading Questions: These contain multiple-choice options. These are almost always more than 10 words. These can be perceived as controlling and tend to limit, end or shut down the conversational flow. They "lead the witness" and frequently result in people selecting a choice from the options you've provided, even when there are more choices. These must be used very carefully, as we'll discuss later in this chapter.

Locking Questions: These elicit a yes or no answer. They are more effective when they are less than 10 words so they don't lose or confuse the customer. They evoke the customer's preference but don't draw out much detail or insight. These can be used to elicit a commitment.

The Proper Use of *Launching, Leading, and Locking Questions*

"Let's give 'em about something to talk about."
– Bonnie Raitt, song title

Let's take a look at how Cho could have approached the conversation. Remember, the goal of *Launching Questions* is to give the two of you "something to talk about."

Launching Question: "What type of employment arrangement would you prefer?"

Leading Question: "Are you interested in a temp or full time position?"

Locking Question: "Would you like a temp job?"

In yoga, we look for a balance between mind and body to create the exquisite experience of "flow." In *Sales Yoga*, our goal is to create a balanced, two-way conversation where there is a flow of questions and insights.

This conversational flow is best achieved by starting "wide-open" with *Launching Questions* that gather information that is important to your customer. As you learn what's imperative to them, you *integrate* the gathered information into your next question.

When you develop a thorough understanding of the customer, their needs, and objectives, you facilitate, with more *Launching Questions*, an agreement on a next course of action, such as the next meeting, a demonstration of your product or service, or the creation of a proposal. *Locking* or *Leading Questions* are used only to confirm details or gain a commitment to the agreed upon next step.

A consulting client once asked me, "Is there a recommended proportion of when and how much to use the different 'L' questions?"

I told her, "Good question. Like yoga, there's no one right answer; no set formula that works for everyone, all the time. Like yoga, it's important to adapt our approach to each situation and person."

She said, "Could you just give me an idea as to a good ratio?"

"Sure. This isn't set in stone, however you're welcome to use it as a guide. The majority of salespeople use more *Leading* and *Locking Questions*. That's why they're perceived as being forceful, controlling and coercive.

I suggest Sales Yogis use up to 95% *Launching Questions* and no more than 5% *Leading* and *Locking Questions*. That creates a collaborative flow and keeps the focus where it belongs—which is on drawing out what matters to the client."

Here's how it might sound in a health club:

Sales *Force* Approach:

A new customer walks in the door. "Hi, I'm interested in yoga!"

The person behind the counter says, "Great, how about tonight at 6 pm or tomorrow morning at 7 am?"

The customer's face falls. "Bummer, I can't make either one. Don't you have any this afternoon? I was kind of hoping to get started today."

"Nope. The only one we have today is that one that starts at 6 pm."

"Oh well. Thanks anyway."

Sales *Flow* Approach:

A new customer walks in the door. "Hi, I'm interested in yoga!"

The person behind the counter asks, "Great! What interests you about yoga?"

"Well," the student replies, "I have a really stressful job. I need to do something about it."

"Okay, tell me about your stress."

"I work in a call center handling customer complaints. I sit all day long. My neck and shoulders are so tight, plus I keep seeing all these studies that say sitting too much leads to all kinds of health problems so I've got to start getting some physical activity."

"What kind of physical activity are you looking for?"

"Well, something vigorous, I want to get my heart rate up."

"Okay, we have some yoga classes that can definitely do that. Before we go into options, what else should I know about your preferences?"

"I've never done yoga before so I'm a little self-conscious about it. I was wondering if you have any personal yoga trainers? I thought maybe I could try a one-on-one session to see if it's for me?"

"Yes, we have a couple of excellent teachers who work privately with clients...."

You can see how the *Sales Flow* approach is much more likely to lead to a "yes" and a mutually beneficial relationship. The *Launching Questions* clarify her objectives, circumstances, and challenges. Now that we know what she needs, we can tailor our recommendations to exactly what she's looking for.

She will walk away feeling listened to and taken care of. The health club is more likely to gain a new customer, and a more valuable one at that, because she was involved in the process of choosing her course of action instead of being handed options— none of which worked for her.

Think about a recent sales experience where you did *not* get the deal. In retrospect, could you have gotten that "No thanks" because you asked *Leading* or *Locking Questions* that unnecessarily limited the conversation?

What is a situation this week where you'll be meeting with a prospective client? How are you going to hold yourself accountable for asking *Launching Questions* that set up *Sales Flow*? How are you going to draw out *what* they need and *why*...instead of offering limited options which might not suit their needs? Increase your likelihood of a win-win outcome by *launching* a two-way interaction that focuses on *their* interests.

Action Plan for Chapter 4

"When are you going to realize that if it doesn't apply to me; it doesn't matter?" – Candace Bergen, in TV sitcom Murphy Brown

For this action plan, vow to work together with staff or colleagues to brainstorm and strategize a series of *Launching, Leading,* and *Locking Questions* to add to your repertoire.

Identify at least three different types of prospective clients you and your team deal with. Your goal is to generate at least five samples of each type of question so you have them in your mental hip pocket. For this exercise, it is not necessary to memorize these and resort to a robotic-like use of them that is not genuine or authentic. I am recommending that if you think about this ahead of time; you'll be better able to think on your feet (and seat) and ask tailored questions in the moment that apply to your customer.

You might want to think of yourself as a *Sales Yoga* detective. Your goal is to draw out and then listen to what your buyer is saying so you have a clear, detailed picture of what they are looking for *before* you offer options. You want to learn as much as you can, including things your buyer may not have realized until you asked provocative questions that crystallized this for them for the first time.

Remember, **Launching Questions** are always open-ended, 10 words or less and cannot be answered with a yes or no. They are your Sales Detective questions.

Leading Questions, when used effectively, contain *strategically-selected,* multiple-choice options and your customer is meant to select an option from the tailored ones you've provided, *based upon their specific needs.* **Locking Questions** elicit a yes or no answer and can be used to elicit a commitment.

Chapter 5:
E = Emphasize Value, Not Price

"What is a cynic? Someone who knows the price of everything and the value of nothing."

– Oscar Wilde

Oscar Wilde had a good point. As *Sales Yoga* practitioners, our goal is to help our customers understand the value of what we're offering so the price is no longer an objection. Gita is a wonderful example of someone who learned how to emphasize the value she was delivering so her customer felt price was secondary.

Gita was a sales manager for a large equipment manufacturing company in the Midwest. They had hired me to advise them on how to realign their sales process. During the project, we discussed the negotiations with one of their long-term clients and their contact Ted, who was head of Procurement.

Gita called me in a panic one day and said, "Ted just called to say it's down to us and another vender; but the other vendor has come in with a lower bid. He wants to know if we'll match it. Now what?"

Gita's first thought was to simply lower her price. This was a multi-million dollar account and she didn't want to risk losing the deal.

I told her, "Gita, I understand you want this account, but lowering your price isn't smart. If you lower your price without removing value, it sends the message to Ted and his company that you had originally presented an inflated amount. The implication is you're gouging them and have built in a huge profit cushion."

"I don't want to send that message, but I don't know what to do instead."

"Okay Gita, here's what we know. If the other vendor's deal was so much better than yours, they would have just taken it instead of calling you back. It's easy to forget this when there's a lot of money on the line, however, your best move it to give them more reasons to buy instead of lowering the price."

"Okay, how do we do that?"

"First, tell me a little more about your conversation with Ted. What do we know about the vendor? What new info did Ted give about what's going on with them?"

"It's interesting you brought that up. Based on your previous advice, I asked some *Launching Questions* and took notes on what he said instead of just assuming it was all about price. He mentioned that this other vendor has more international experience, but that wasn't a requirement on the original proposal."

"Perfect. I suggest you get back to him with three options. Option One is going to be a lower price; but you're going to take away a few deliverables that aren't crucial. Option Two is the first bid you submitted. That way if it really IS about saving money and taking the lowest bid, you'll get the deal.

Also submit an Option Three that has a *higher* price, but that includes an added project manager who has an impressive track record of international leadership."

Gita pushed back a bit, "Scott, they asked me to *lower* the price, not *raise* it."

"You're right. However, remember, if the other vendor's option had been that much better, we wouldn't be having this conversation. Sounds to me you're still in the game if you focus on meeting the needs he told you they value."

Gita agreed and presented the three options to Ted. She called me the following Monday and said, "Scott, you're not going to believe this. Actually, you probably are going to believe it because you predicted it. They are going with Option Three. He said it's worth the extra money because he'd researched our international guy's credentials and found out he's led this type of product launch before and brought it in under budget and before the deadline and that's what they want."

Good for Gita for understanding that value trumps price. If you can find out what your client values—and if you clarify how you and your company will honor that and deliver that—then price becomes a secondary issue.

Here is another example. Many of my consultant colleagues travel for business. Most of them belong to premier clubs of their favorite airline, hotel chain and rental car agency.

One of them was complaining to me recently about how much it had cost her to fly cross-country to speak at a conference for nonprofit leaders. She told me, "My client didn't pick up expenses so this trip cost me almost $1000 out of pocket."

"Why did it cost so much? I've seen fares on Expedia or Travelocity for a lot less than that."

"I know…but those package flights are usually on Southwest or something like that…and I wouldn't get my points."

"You mean you rather pay a few hundred extra dollars just to get mileage points?"

"Well, it's not just that. I don't have to wait in line at the airport for my flight or rental car, and I usually get upgraded to business class on the plane and to the concierge floor at the hotel."

Clearly, my friend Sandra values "head of the line" service, legroom and higher-quality accommodations than she does saving money and getting the lowest price.

How about you? Where in your life is price not *an* issue—or not *the* issue?

Realtors know that purchasing the lowest-priced house is not what drives most homebuyers. That's why they spend a lot of time finding out what matters to you. View of the lake? Modern kitchen with state-of-the-art appliances? Man-cave to watch football? A room that can be turned into a nursery? A backyard with a garden?

People are willing to pay for what they value. Our goal is to meet their needs while delivering tremendous value that makes it worth paying our price.

So, if you're selling a proposal, product or program and it's being challenged on price, understand that price is really *not* the issue. The issue is, you haven't yet demonstrated that you're delivering enough value that meets their needs for them to say yes.

Here are seven questions to ask that can help identify what your customer values:

---

1. **What does the customer want to achieve?** What are their goals? Lose 20 lbs? Be the #1 store in this mall? Have a quality website up? Be an INC 500 winner?
2. **What is their ideal time frame to achieve this?** 1 week? 1 month? 1 year?
3. **Why is this important to them?** Health? Status? Profits? Reputation?
4. **What are fears, doubts, concerns they have about this?** Afraid to fail? Had a bad experience before? Worried it will take too long? Not sure it will be an ROI?

5. **What problems or issues do they have they want solved?** In danger of losing market share? Mounting medical bills? Losing customers?

6. **Who is impacting their decision and how?** Partner is sabotaging? They're not the final decision maker? Team members are conflicted? Family member is sick?

7. **What specific, positive consequences will they receive?** What else do they value, want, and need more than money that will make this worthwhile? Legacy? Being around for grandchildren? Dividend for shareholders?

Have the Courage to be Uncommon

"When you can do a common thing in an uncommon way; you will command the attention of the world."
– George Washington Carver

Many salespeople compete on price. It's a crowded space. It's the least sophisticated way to sell. Still, the majority of salespeople fall back on this technique when they're afraid of losing a deal.

Get clear, once and for all…*the lowest price rarely means the best investment.*

Sales Yogis emphasize value, not price. If you ask *Launching Questions* and practice *Mind Over Mouth*, you'll be able to identify what your customers genuinely care about. If you take the time and make the effort to answer the seven questions above, you'll be able to identify what your customers need and value.

And when you're clear about what your customers value; you'll be able to offer options they value. At that point, as long as your price is reasonable; they'll feel it's a good value…and you've got yourself a deal.

Action Plan for Chapter 5

"Anything that just costs money is cheap."
– John Steinbeck

In yoga, there are elements, such as posture, breathing, and focus that are part of the foundations of the practice. In the process of S.A.L.E.S. Y.O.G.A. you are learning that *HalfTalk*, a Do-Over Mentality, *Launching Questions*, and emphasizing value over price are your foundations for distinguishing yourself in the hearts and minds of buyers.

Think of a recent sale you made, one in which the focal point was money. Recall some of your conversations with that client. Did the majority of your discussions involve payment plans, discounts, commissions, the going price or your competitor's fee?

Ask yourself, "Did I ask the seven questions to find out what my client genuinely valued? Did I take the time to explore what else they cared about? Did I really listen to what was said — and what was unsaid? Did I uncover other opinions or interests that could have made price a non-issue? In retrospect, could it have been to my advantage to draft and submit three different price/ value options?"

Let's reverse-engineer what could have happened if you had come in with three alternatives. Fill out the grid below. Speculate about some unexpected options you might have offered. Project what other interests they might have had that didn't come up in your conversation. Might your customer have been willing to explore other options if they'd known they were available? Is it possible you left money on the table? Could you promise yourself to offer three options to your *next* client so they make their decision on value, not price?

Option	Deliverables and Reduced or Added Value	Price
#1		
#2		
#3		

Chapter 6:
S = Shields Up or Shields Down?

"Energy is the key to creativity. Energy is the key to life."

– William Shatner

The sales world can be rough.

Many customers are leery and weary. Leery of manipulative sales tactics and weary of unethical salespeople who only care about closing the sale. As a result, many have developed automatic "Just looking" responses to protect themselves from unwanted sales pitches.

Are you a Trekkie? A good friend is and she tells me that in the popular *Star Trek* series, every episode introduces some kind of threat to the Starship Enterprise. When that threat occurs, Captain Kirk immediately orders "Shields Up" to protect the vessel and minimize any potential damage. The shield even has all kinds of gee-whiz modifications depending on the kind of attack they're under.

Because of the negative reputation of salespeople, many buyers have developed their own version of "Shields Up" to ward off unwanted sales "attacks." These responses are meant to keep us at a distance and throw us off the sales trail. Here are 10 basic "Sales Shields" you might have encountered (or deployed yourself). Once we identify them, we'll discuss creative ways to change people's negative energy into positive energy so they're more open to what we have to offer.

10 Sales Shields

Shield #1: *"No thanks; just looking."*

Imagine you walk into a department store, looking for a new outfit. After wandering through a few sections, you see some things you like and start pulling out clothes to try on. Out of the corner of your eye you spot movement; a sales clerk is heading your way. She closes in on you and you prepare yourself for the inevitable question. "Hi, can I help you find something?" Up goes your shield, "No thanks; just looking."

Shield #2: *Avoidance*

While waiting for some friends at the mall, you spot some interesting housewares items in the display window of a store. You walk in to check them out. Once inside, you notice a sales clerk at the register glancing over at you. You hunch your shoulders, turn your back and you do your best to be invisible. A moment later, you peek over your shoulder to see if she's still checking you out. Yep, there she is, an aisle over, waiting for you to touch something. You quickly avert your eyes and pretend to be uninterested, hoping to not show up on her radar by engaging your personal stealth system.

Shield #3: *"Sorry, he's in a meeting."*

As a salesperson, making phone calls is part of your job. Cold calls, in particular, are challenging as, more often than not, people are not pleased when they realize who is on the other end of the phone. You get a bit suspicious though when, calling a prospect back for the third time, you once again hear the five little words, "Sorry, he's in a meeting."

Shield #4: *"No Soliciting"*

You drop in on a potential customer to introduce yourself and leave some literature.

You walk in through the heavy glass doors and make your way to the lobby desk with a smile on your face. Without even saying a word, the receptionist rolls her eyes and impatiently points to a sign that says in large letters, "No Soliciting."

Shield #5: *Hiding Out*

'Fess up. Have you ever hidden in another room when the doorbell rang and you knew it was a salesman? I have. I get it. My time at home is so precious, I don't want to spend it having to explain to a salesperson why I'm not interested in his or her product or service. And I don't want to be rude because I know what it's like to be on the receiving end of that. Easier just to pretend no one's home.

My friend Bob, owner of a small printing company in Florida, told me he often employs this strategy at work. His office is located next to the lobby, which allows him to eavesdrop when someone asks to see him. Any time it's an uninvited salesperson, his receptionist has been instructed to say, "Bob's not here." Bob told me, "To be safe, I don't leave my office until I'm sure the salesperson has left the building…but I prefer to hide out rather than deal with the disappointment on their face."

Shield #6: *Hanging Up*

Some people don't mess around. The second they realize a caller is trying to sell something, they disconnect the phone. Some of them don't even bother to say, "Not interested," or "Thanks, but no thanks."

I'll always remember what a cab driver told me about this. He picked me up at my hotel and took me to the Denver airport. If you've ever made that trip, it's a l-o-n-g drive from downtown, so he started a conversation. "What type of work do you do?"

"I'm a consultant and speaker, along with delivering workshops for sales teams."

He snorted and said, "I hope you don't train those telemarketers. I hate it when they call right in the middle of dinner or interrupt my favorite TV show. I'm even on a Do Not Call list, but they still track me down somehow. I've come up with a way to keep them from ruining my evening though.

"I call it 'The Nice Guy's Hang Up.' Here's how it works. I'll listen until they ask me a question. I say a few words and then hang-up mid-sentence. It makes it seem like we've been disconnected because no one hangs up on himself."

Looking rather pleased with himself, the cabbie added, "And if they do call back, I don't answer. That makes it look like there's trouble with the line."

Have You Been on the Receiving End of Any of These Sales Shields?

"The shields are dropping." – Joachim
"Then raise them." – Khan
"I can't." – Joachim
"Where's the override?" – Khan (from Star Trek II: Wrath of Khan)

Let's take a mini-break for a moment.

Are you feeling a little discouraged? With so many defenses, it's a wonder any sales are made at all.

This is why it is our responsibility as *Sales Yoga* practitioners to adjust our approach. This does not mean we come up with sneaky ways to get around these shields. We come up with legitimate ways to remove or override the *reason* for the shields so prospective customers feel more comfortable, safe and genuinely engaged.

I was talking about this Star Trek-motivated "Sales Shields" idea with a client named Jean, who is an account manager for an employment agency in Massachusetts. She agreed immediately that Sales Shields are a real challenge. "Oh, yes, I run into these every week. I call anywhere between 50-60 companies a day to see if they're short-staffed and explore other ways I can be of service. Believe me, it's a challenge to get even a few minutes of people's time these days, much less an appointment. In fact, there are a few more shields you might want to add to the list."

"There are more?!" I asked in mock horror.

"Oh yes." And then she added four more Sales Shields

Maximum Shields! Shield #7: *Deferment*

- "I'll have to run this by my boss."
- "I can't make a decision until I discuss it with my spouse."
- "Our buyer's in charge of this. Give me your number and I'll have her call you back when she's available."
- "Send me some information, and I'll give it some thought."

Do any of the above sound familiar? While it's often true that people need to involve someone else in a buying decision, deferment provides an immediate out and gives people a legitimate excuse or justifiable reason for saying, "Not interested."

Shield #8: *Legal Hurdles*

The National Do-Not-Call Registry enacted in 2003 in the U.S. is just one example of legislation that has seriously impacted— and not for the better—everyone selling products and services. All people have to do is add their name to the list to "opt out" of receiving "robo-calls" or any outreach from telemarketers. The ripple effect of this law is felt far beyond the telemarketing industry. A client told me his "potential contact" list plummeted 78% the week following the enacting of this policy. Now *that's* an obstacle.

Shield #9: *Little White Lies*

Some people don't want to hurt the salesperson's feelings so they construct fabrications they hope will end the conversation without being "mean." Perhaps you've heard or said some of the following:

- "We just bought one."
- "I can't afford that right now."
- "They don't live here anymore."
- "That's not in our budget."

Shield #10: *Technical Wonders*

If salespeople were the main characters in *The Wizard of Oz*, instead of chanting, "Lions and tigers and bears, oh my," they'd repeat something like, "Spam Filters and TeleZappers and Call Block, oh my."

If you're not familiar with the technical innovations designed to shield consumers from selling, here are a few examples:

TeleZapper – According to the manufacturers of the TeleZapper, this product "uses the technology of telemarketers' automatic dialing equipment *against* them. When your answering machine picks up a call, the TeleZapper emits a special tone that 'fools' the computer into thinking your number is disconnected. Instead of connecting you to a salesperson, the computer drops the call and stores your number as disconnected in its database."

Spam Filters – This software helps stop spam from entering your email inbox. These programs employ a list of keywords commonly used in spam to "kill" the message before it ever reaches you.

Call Block – With a touch of a few keys, people can block your phone number, permanently keeping you from calling them again from that line.

Call Screening – This feature is available on a growing number of automated phone attendant services used primarily by small businesses. Callers are required to speak their name before being transferred. The person you're calling hears your recorded name and has the option of accepting or rejecting your call.

Caller ID – Do you check Caller ID *first* before answering your phone? Well, so do many of your prospective buyers.

After reviewing all 10 Sales Shields with Jean, she said, "No wonder I feel so drained at the end of the day. That's a daunting list. After bumping into these all day, every day, I sometimes think I might as well quit."

Jean has a point. It does seem the odds are stacked against salespeople these days. The good news is, there are *ethical* ways to engage with potential customers that motivate them to drop their automatic Sales Shields. Here are a few examples.

Shield #1: *"No Thank you, Just looking."*	Acknowledge their comment and gently ask a different question, such as "Of course, I understand. I'm just curious; what was it about our store that caught your attention?"
Shield #2: *Avoidance*	Demonstrate your awareness of what you perceive from their body language with a statement like, "You look like you'd rather not be stalked by a salesperson. My name is Scott and I'll be over at the desk if you have any questions."

Shield #3: *"Sorry, he's in a meeting."*	Ring him back early morning or late afternoon when his assistant has gone home and he's more likely to answer his own phone.
Shield #4: *No Soliciting*	Start with a telephone call. If the same receptionist who greeted you at the door answers the phone, ask for accounts receivable. Calls are rarely screened for that department and you can ask for their help to get to the buyer.

Are you tired of trying to navigate around Sales Shields? So is your team. At your next staff meeting, ask everyone to identify the Sales Shields they encounter most often. Ask everyone to put themselves in the shoes of their prospective customers so they understand how they feel. Acknowledge that your customers are busy and don't like to be interrupted in the middle of a workday or a rare evening at home.

What would you like to hear that is so gracious, you would be inspired to "take the call" or spend a few minutes finding out more about the salesperson's offer? What would be a non-invasive outreach you could use that would motivate someone to give you a few moments of his or her valuable time and mind?

In case you're wondering what yoga has taught me about shields, it's this. I still run into someone, every once in a while, who thinks yoga is a "sissy" (their words, not mine) sport.

In fact, I was at a conference recently, sharing drinks with a couple consultants from the other side of the country. We started swapping tips about how we stay in shape when we're on the road so much traveling. Tim told me he was a former football player and keeps fit with frequent trips to the gym. He lifts weights and has the muscles to show for it.

When I told him I keep in shape with yoga, he laughed and said, "You've got to be kidding." He dismissed yoga as not having any value for strength training. His shields were definitely up. Instead of arguing, I asked with a smile, "Willing to try something that shows that yoga is a form of strength training?"

"Sure," he said, clearly not expecting much.

I said, "Have you ever done a 'wall sit?' Let's both put our back against the wall, and slide down until it looks like we're sitting on a chair...but there's no chair there."

"Sure," he scoffed. I could tell he thought this would be no contest.

We both assumed our "wall sit" positions. After about 30 seconds, I could see a tremble in his quads. I could also tell he was determined to win and not let me see him sweat. After about 60 seconds, he was groaning out loud and couldn't hide the shake in his legs. He finally collapsed after about 80 seconds. Between you and me, I was glad he did because I only had a few more seconds left in my legs.

He said, with begrudging respect in his voice, "Okay, I admit that yoga is a form of strength training." We had a nice conversation and he even admitted he was going to give yoga a try. Voilà...shields down!

Action Plan for Chapter 6

"Never change a winning game; always change a losing one." – Coach Vince Lombardi

Now it's your turn. Draft some responses to the following list of Sales Shields that might motivate a prospective customer to give you a chance. What could get those Sales Shields down instead of up?

As Coach Lombardi pointed out, if you're losing, it's time to change your approach. Ask yourself, what would connect with me? What could someone say that would intrigue me and win my attention…even if just for a few moments? Take a few moments to write down your responses so you can use them next time someone's about to say "Just browsing" or "No thanks."

Shield #5: *Hiding Out*

Shield #6: *Hanging Up*

Shield #7: *Hanging Up*

Shield #8: *Legal Hurdles*

Shield #9: *Little White Lies*

Shield #10: *Technical Wonders*

Chapter 7:
Y = Yet

"You miss 100% of the shots you never take."

– Wayne Gretzky

At a recent workshop on the west coast, I was asked about one of the biggest challenges we salespeople face. The ballroom of our hotel was packed with 300 people. It was just after our mid-morning break and I'd opened it up for Q & A. One young woman, Michelle, raised her hand and said, "I can see that your techniques work when people need what we're selling; but what if they *don't* need what we're selling?"

I could tell the audience was kind of surprised she asked this...however it's something we all need to deal with. I smiled and said..."*Create the Yet!*"

Michelle looked at me, obviously puzzled and said, "Create the Yet?"

I asked if she'd be willing to come up to the front of the room so we could demonstrate what I was talking about. We created a scenario in which she was the manager at a 3PL (Third Party

Logistics) company. (An example of such a company would be Old Dominion Trucking, which moves freight.)

I said, "Okay, Michelle, you and I are going to role-play a meeting that we've scheduled. The purpose is to determine how I can be of a service."

"First, know that I've done my homework. I studied your company website and Google'd it to see if it's been in the news. I wanted to see if you've won an award, or you're dealing with layoffs, or if your CEO was just interviewed in a national publication. Maybe an industry journal reported about major changes taking place in your industry. Maybe you're expanding overseas. All of this 'advance work' has helped me prepare so I can walk in with confidence because I know I have a lot of Yet's I can create.

"Now, 2 minutes into our meeting, after exchanging hellos, you say, 'I'm sorry Scott, we really just don't require your services. We're pretty well covered. Thanks for stopping by.'"

"I say, "I understand, Michelle. I'm curious about something. I read in *Investors Business Daily* about some recent regulations affecting your industry. The article quoted (a CFO of a competing company) and he voiced some concern about their potential impact. I'm curious as to your thoughts about this and if you agree with what he said?'"

Michelle took a moment to think. I could see she was trying to work this out in her mind so I let her take her time. I appreciated how seriously she was taking this scenario.

Finally, she leaned toward me and said, "You know, Scott, we *are* concerned about these regulations. And to be quite honest, we're not really sure what we're going to do. I'm afraid we're going to have to cut back on some of our personnel."

"I see, and where do you think you'll do that?"

"I'm not really sure at this point."

I could see Michelle was intrigued. From her perspective, this certainly wasn't the traditional "hard-sell" approach and she wanted to know where I was going with this.

Now, the ball was in my court to *earn* her attention, respect and business by presenting her with something she and her company would value that they didn't expect.

"Well, what if there was a way to reduce your costs by outsourcing some of the work that is currently being done in-house?"

"Keep talking, Scott, I'd like to hear how you'd propose to do that."

"I'd be glad to show you some options that could help mitigate the impact of these regulations. I would just need to ask you some additional questions?"

"Why don't we set up another meeting? I don't have time right now; but I know my team would be interested to hear innovative ways for us to address this."

Michelle "pulled out" of the role-play and said, "Wow, I see what you mean. I went from telling you 'No thanks' two minutes into our conversation to requesting another meeting."

I told her, "Exactly. See how doing our homework and finding pending problems our prospect will be facing in the near future can help them see that while they may not need our services *right now*...they may very well need them in the months ahead when these challenges materialize?"

Our job is to figure out what circumstances might cause our prospect to need us in the future. What factors are going to influence them? What might they not even be aware of—that we can help them with a month or more down the road?

What was really interesting about this role-play with Michelle was that the whole thing was a fabricated scenario in front of an audience. *Yet*, (ha ha) the audience was sitting on the edge of their seats, riveted. They were invested in seeing where the conversation went because we've all been turned down flat by clients who didn't perceive we had anything of value to offer them... and wanted to know what they could do when that happens.

During the debriefing, Michelle admitted to me and the group that she had initially planned on finding a way to shut me down. A manager would do that, too! But, she didn't want to once we started talking because she wanted to know "the rest of the story."

I asked the group: "Now, let's be realistic. Is Michelle ready to buy at this point?"

"*NOT YET!*" they yelled.

"Exactly. Our goal here was to get another chance to continue the conversation. That's what Creating a Yet does. Instead of 'Game Over,' we got another meeting."

So, next time your client is on the verge of telling you they don't need your services, introduce a forthcoming challenge they'll be facing that you've gleaned from your research. It will often result in a "We don't need you…Yet…but I'm intrigued enough to keep the conversation going."

Yoga Is All About the "Yet"

"My new motto is, 'When you're through changing, you're through.'" – Bruce Barton

Every time I go to my yoga class, I'm reminded of the Yet principle. There are a lot of long-time students in my class who are very fit, very flexible, and very strong.

It was rather intimidating in the beginning because I couldn't do some of the poses. I was fortunate to have a wise, patient teacher who could see my frustration. We were doing a plank. Well, the people around me were doing a plank. I was doing my version of a plank, which consisted of a somewhat kneeled version of a push up. My back was bothering me and I couldn't hold the pose as long as others in the class. After collapsing for the third time, she came over to offer support. I said in disgust, "It's hopeless. I can't do plank for that long."

She said gently, "*Yet.* You can't do that *yet.*"

Aahh. She's right. Giving up never accomplished anything. Concluding something is a lost cause turns that belief into a self-fulfilling prophecy.

Yoga is about continuing to try. Continuing to apply. About embracing change instead of being through with it.

Thanks to that Yet philosophy, guess who can now hold a plank for long periods of time? Thanks to that Yet philosophy, guess who has created many mutually prosperous relationships that otherwise would have ended at the first "We don't need your services?"

The Yet philosophy is one of the most important principles of *Sales Yoga* because it positively impacts us in so many ways. You might even want to do what one of my consulting clients did. Lynda told me, "You know how we go to workshops and leave all fired up, ready to change the world? Then, a couple days later, everything is back to same-old, same-old?

"I didn't want that to happen this time so I put an index card up on my refrigerator that said 'Yet.' I put one on my desk, one on my iPad cover and one on the inside of my notebook that I take with me to all my appointments. I get more second meetings now thanks to keeping that Yet in-sight, in-mind."

Action Plan for Chapter 7

"I've heard every excuse on the planet— except a good one." – Bob Greene

First, let's reflect.

- When was the last time a customer told you they didn't need your services?
- How did it feel when you heard the dreaded "Thanks, but no thanks?"

- In retrospect, did you do your homework? Did your research reveal some upcoming challenge or opportunity that would be impacting this company and customer?
- Could you have introduced some scenarios that could have created a Yet?

Now, let's look ahead. What prospective customer will you be reaching out to this week? How can you increase your likelihood of success by creating a Yet? Don't accept excuses and don't give them. Come up with options that open up possibilities.

- How are you going to research this company? Are you going to study their website? Google them? Study their YouTube Channel or Yelp reviews?
- How are you going to identify challenges or opportunities their industry will be facing in the upcoming year? Are you going to read industry journals or check out their professional association's website? Explain.
- How are you going to identify at least three different problems this organization could be facing that could help them with…if not now, in the months ahead?
- How are you going to diplomatically introduce your Yet's so your contact is sufficiently intrigued to request another meeting or follow-up call?

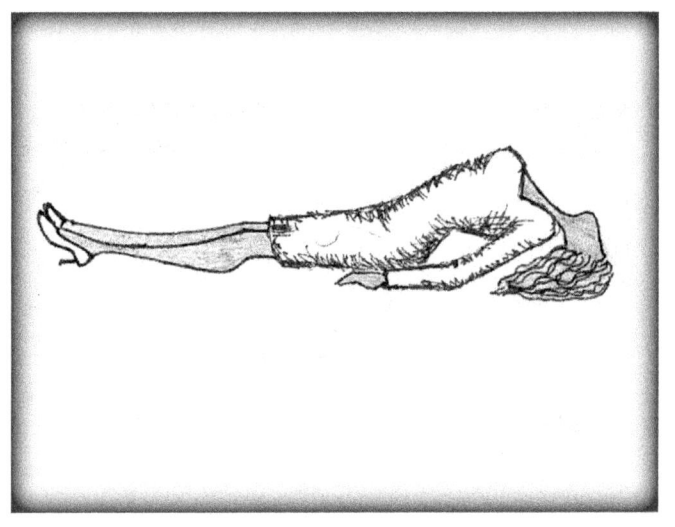

Chapter 8:
O = Objections are Opportunities

"Obstacles are those things you see when you take your eyes off your goal."

– coffee mug slogan

In the previous chapter on Yet we talked about how to do our homework and introduce unanticipated options that have the power to transform a "no" into a "not yet."

As mentioned, that approach is another foundation of *Sales Yoga* success. It reminds us to be open to possibility and opportunities instead of prematurely concluding we're doomed to fail.

I tell my clients I LOVE the opportunities created by objections. If I can find out *why* someone is about to turn me down; then it's just a matter of me being smart enough and creative enough to figure out how to address those objections so they're no longer an issue. *It's like getting the test in advance.* They're giving us the answers by saying, "THIS is why I don't want to do business with you." Now, it's just a matter of making that resistance moot by asking *Launching Questions* to fully understand the objection so, together, we can remove or change the aspects that are bothering them.

I believe most sales are salvageable—*as long as we see objections as opportunities.*

A colleague graduated with an MBA from Stanford. Denise believes in negotiating everything. She doesn't take no for an answer. She is definitely a walking, talking example and lead proponent of the "not Yet" philosophy.

To celebrate getting her degree, she decided to "Feng Shui" her home. Out with the old and in with the new. After cleaning out every closet and getting rid of everything that wasn't beautiful, functional or meaningful; she went furniture shopping with her interior designer. She found exactly what she wanted—a matching living room, dining room, and bedroom set—at the first store they went to. She told the salesperson she was ready to buy everything on the spot and asked, "How soon can this be delivered?"

The sales clerk said, "Let me see if we have everything in stock, but delivery time is normally six to eight weeks."

Denise couldn't believe what she was hearing. "Six to eight weeks?! I was hoping to get it tomorrow."

"Oh, there's no way we could get this to you tomorrow. First, we have to get it from the manufacturer and they usually make partial shipments as items become available."

This was a deal-breaker for Denise; but then her "objections are opportunities" mind-set kicked in. She realized they'd hadn't gotten creative and explored options yet.

"Isn't there any way I can get this furniture sooner? I've got an empty house. I donated everything to Salvation Army. I don't have anything to eat on, sit on, or sleep on."

The sales clerk shrugged her shoulders, thinking they were at a dead end. She obviously didn't know Denise. Denise wasn't deterred by the clerk's objections. She was clear they hadn't explored enough options…yet. If they did, it was only a matter of time before they came up with a win-win solution.

Then, it occurred to her. "What about the floor models? They have a few scratches and stuff…but I'll buy them if you can give me a modest discount and they can be delivered by this weekend."

Bingo. She had herself a deal.

How about you? Do you accept the first objection as your final answer…or do you see it as an opportunity to get creative and keep generating other possibilities?

In this case, it was the buyer who facilitated the solution, not the salesperson, which supports a premise of this book that buyers and sellers are equals. The good news is, you can use *Sales Yoga* techniques to produce a better outcome in both roles. The point is, instead of giving up and declaring something a lost cause when someone raises an objection, keep the conversation going.

A friend was the beneficiary of a salesperson who kept the conversation going. My friend travels a lot as part of her business. She says, "I know I should exercise more, but I'm on the road so much, the last thing I want to do when I get home is go to the gym."

Her son said, "Mom, why don't you hire a personal trainer? They can come to the house. You don't even have to get in the car. They bring everything to you."

She agreed she needed to do something to get back into shape and called a home fitness organization. All was going well until the personal trainer revealed her rates. "Wow," my friend said, "that's almost $100 an hour. That's a lot of money."

Instead of arguing with her, the personal trainer asked some *Launching Questions* to better understand the concerns around price. Equipped with a better understanding of the issues, she then said, "You're right, $100 is a lot of money. And let me tell you what one of my clients told me. At this time last year, she was 60 pounds overweight, was taking insulin for diabetes, and had a hard time walking because her knees hurt so much. My client told me, 'I now weigh the same I did in college, no longer have to take insulin, can comfortably jog two miles…and nothing hurts."

She told me she pays LESS than she used to pay for insulin and doctor visits and considers our time together the single best investment she's made in her health and quality of life.

My friend was sold, and is now enjoying the benefits of 3x a week workouts. Good thing that personal trainer didn't stop at the first objection!

Don't Let a NO Stop Your *Sales Flow*

"Understand that every time you say no to one thing; you say yes to something else." – Maggie Bedrosian

While it's important to continue the conversation after the first objection, it's also important to prepare for those times when "no" really does mean "no."

As an honorable Sales Yogi, our job is to make peace with those "final answers" and turn to the next opportunity with the same enthusiasm and confidence we started with. And, that is often easier said than done.

Early in my sales career, I worked mostly by phone. As we all know, in order to make a sale, you have to make lots of phone calls and the majority of them will not be returned. Buyers only return phone calls when they feel it's in their best interests to do so. One of the things that got me through those long, tedious days of "no" was a firm belief that I would not hear "no" forever.

Whether the buyer chose not to call back or told me "no thanks" after our conversation, those both qualified as rejections. So, in order to stay motivated, I had to realize that every "no" meant I was that much closer to the next "yes."

It is statistically improbable that even the most average salesperson in the world will hear "no" forever. Eventually, we catch someone at the right time with the right need and close the deal. It's only a matter of time. I decided that "no" isn't really a word, it's an acronym. **NO means Next Opportunity.**

People who were turning me down or turning me away were actually saying two things to me:

- **First,** I need to move on to my next opportunity because, for whatever reason, they don't perceive this as a win-win, which means they aren't the right opportunity for either of us, right now.
- **Second,** there will be another opportunity to talk with them in the future because circumstances change, which means "no", *is not a permanent condition.*

I call this willingness to move from one call to the next, from one opportunity to the next...*Sales Flow.*

Sales Flow is essential to our personal and professional well-being. In yoga, the smooth transition between poses is what makes yoga such a soothing experience.

In each pose you focus on quieting your mind, maximizing your energy, stretching your body to its limits...while maintaining balance and breath. As you transition from one pose to the next, you release the previous pose and give your full attention to the next pose. That's an essential element of flow, let go, move on. Let go, move on.

Did you see the movie *A League of Their Own* with Gina Davis, Tom Hanks, and Madonna? Remember the famous line, *"There's no crying in baseball?"*

Well, there's no holding grudges in yoga.

And there's no holding grudges in Sales Yoga, either!

Rather than becoming frustrated or angry at receiving a "no," you let go. You ground yourself in your original purpose and move ahead.

For example, in yoga if you're going to do Tree Pose, before you ever take a foot off the floor you must be clear on where your support comes from. Let's say I'm going to do Tree Pose with my right foot grounded and my left foot up.

The first thing I'm going to do is put my focus on my right foot and spread my toes as much as possible, grounding into the floor and visualizing myself rooted to the ground. I will wait until I feel the support of the ground through my right foot before lifting my left into the Tree Pose position.

I may wobble a bit, which is fine. The wobble will go away in time as long as I persistently practice grounding myself. The wobble doesn't come from the difficulty of the pose, it comes from my inconsistent focus and commitment to preparation and repetition.

The better I become at staying grounded, the smoother the flow of the pose becomes. Then and only then will I center my gaze on a focal point, straight ahead and position my left foot against my right knee.

In *Sales Yoga*, you ground yourself, first and foremost, by remembering who you are. Remember why you are there and what tremendous value you can provide to your customers. These points of focus will steady you through the wobble of hearing "no."

Accepting a No with Grace

"If you're not willing to lose, then you'll do whatever it takes to win, and you become someone you don't want to be."
– Katie Couric

Several of our *Sales Yoga* techniques explore how to change a "no" into a "not yet," and how to get creative in coming up with previously unknown needs so we can continue the conversation and ultimately get a deal. This particular chapter suggests that we see objections as opportunities and persevere to get what we want—instead of giving up when we're initially told a deal is not going to happen.

As long as we do this *ethically* and with the goal of producing a *mutually rewarding* relationship, gentle persistence can be a win for all involved.

As Katie Couric points out though, this does NOT include acting out of integrity or persevering when it's clear that it's only to our advantage to do so.

In yoga, my teacher constantly reminds us to listen to our body and honor what it can or can't do. Although yoga can be strenuous; it's not supposed to hurt. It's not a failure to give up a pose that is causing us pain. It's smart.

The same with sales. It is not a failure to let go of a relationship, for now, that is causing you pain. Listen to—and honor—your instincts that alert you to something that's just not working. If you have genuinely tried, tried, tried and something doesn't feel "right," it's wrong to persist. Ground yourself in your integrity and your intention to create a win-win. Set up *Sales Flow*. Let go. Move on.

Action Plan for Chapter 8

"You are not what you do; you are what you contribute."
– Columnist Carolyn Hax

Think about a relationship with a prospect or current client where you have repeatedly been told, "No thanks." Have you chosen to see objections as opportunities? Have you persevered through multiple rejections and explored options in an effort to get a yes?

Has it been worth it? Do you still feel there's a chance to produce a mutually rewarding relationship? If so, persevere. If not, maybe it's time to let go, for now, and move on. What feels right? What are your instincts telling you? Take a moment to ground yourself in your Sales Yogi mentality. Consider what your contribution is.

What makes what you do every day worth the effort? What is special, significant and important about what you provide? Take a moment to write these down. Put them on a post-it and or enter them into your smart-phone where you can access them. This is going to be a totem, (discussed in more detail in Chapter 11) that keeps you grounded when you hear a NO (Next Opportunity). Here's an example:

◊   As a Sales Yogi, I:
  o   Operate ethically & with integrity
  o   Am worthy of my customer's trust
  o   Help buyers make win-win decisions.
◊   My company & I provide tremendous value.
◊   NO = Next Opportunity

Chapter 9:
G = Go It Together

"Remember, we're all in this ... alone."

– Lily Tomlin

David is a 40 something owner of a tech consulting company in Texas. His employees were struggling to maintain their motivation and their performance was suffering. David called me in to consult, hoping I'd institute some changes that would breathe life back into their business.

I went in and observed the working environment for a few days and found people working diligently on their computers, either in cubicles or offices, heads down and fingers typing away.

I didn't see anyone collaborating or gathering in the lunchroom for a "coffee break." There was no water cooler chatter because there was no water cooler. In fact, I noticed a distinct lack of interaction between employees. Therein lay the issue.

I met with David to present my findings. "David, your employees are working as hard as they can. They don't appear to be wasting time on gossip binges or bad-mouthing. They're not sneaking on to Facebook, making private phone calls on company time, texting, taking long smoke breaks or hiding in the bathroom."

David looked disappointed despite the seemingly good news, and I knew why. If they weren't wasting time somehow, somewhere…then did it just mean they weren't capable of being more productive? David asked the obvious question,

"Scott, if they're not wasting time, what's causing this? Why are they so…slow?"

"Well, from what I can see, your office could use some small talk!"

David looked shocked so I continued before he could ask for a refund.

"Your employees are so isolated in their cubicles and offices, this place might as well be a one-man show. They come in, sit at their desk, put on their headsets and sell in their own little world. While it seems like they're focused and free of distraction, they actually feel unsupported, disconnected and alone. Sales is *not* a private practice!"

"So what are you saying? Should we have an office party or something?"

"Not exactly…but kind of. I call it *Sellergy*. Here's what I suggest.…"

At 8:00 am the next day, David asked his sales team to come into the conference room. A dozen people filed into the room and settled down with curious looks on their faces. First, we asked the group to go around the room, and each had up to two minutes to talk about something good that had happened to them that month. It could be something from work (a sales quota surpassed or an extension of an annual contract), or it could be something from home, (a brand new puppy, a son who scored the winning run in a Little League game, a 10th year anniversary).

The group was a little taken aback because they had never shared personal information in a staff meeting before. David had always separated business and home. Meetings were kept to a tight agenda and focused exclusively on work issues.

The first people were rather hesitant to share something about their personal life, but then one 20-something said she'd just gotten back from her sister's wedding, which had been held in Hawaii. Another employee said, "I used to live in Hawaii! What island did you go to?"

Another employee said he was training for a triathlon. Allison, who was sitting next to him said, "I'm training for a triathlon too. Where do you do your swims?" They discovered they both worked out at the same health club and didn't even know it.

David said, "Scott, our employees bonded more in that meeting than they have in the three years they've worked for me!"

The next week we had another staff meeting. This time we decided to brainstorm/strategize a list of *Launching Questions* everyone could use. The salespeople realized they weren't sharing "big data" with each other. Everyone was re-creating the wheel, which was probably why the company was suffering a sales slump.

I said, "Want to know a question that almost always elicits information gold?

"The question is, '*How is your business changing?*'

"That almost *always* generates more sales opportunities (Yet's) because it identifies new problems, procedures and policies that aren't being addressed."

Our group generated a list, on our white board, of six new *Launching Questions* no one had used before. We made sure everyone had taken notes and then asked them to go back to their desks to make outgoing prospect calls using these questions. We told them we'd reconvene at 10 am and were looking forward to hearing progress reports.

At 10 o'clock, everyone gathered in the conference room to share one success story and one challenge. This created instant cause for celebration and instant source of accountability.

They were able to immediately learn from each other's example. Everyone also shared feedback and ended up coaching each other on how to fine-tune their approach so they'd be more effective next time.

It also became apparent that a couple of the employees hadn't followed through as they didn't have anything positive to share. Who knows whether it was because they didn't take the assignment seriously or they were having a bad day...but I suggested to David that these two receive coaching and/or counseling to bring them up to speed or to find out whether they were not a fit for a sales position.

We repeated this pattern throughout the day: sales calls with the *Launching Question* focus followed by another debrief, and again, and then again. By the end of the day, we had integrated a full day of selling with education, coaching, accountability, and measureable improvement.

David was ecstatic. Not only had we transformed their bleak sales environment into a dynamic learning environment, his employees came together as a team that genuinely cared about each other. In just a couple short weeks, there was laughter in the halls, something that had been absent before. I saw employees greeting each other by name and going out of their way to ask about the puppy and the triathlon training. There was warmth in the room...where before it had been cold and impersonal.

Turn Your Weekly Staff Meetings into *Sellergy* Meetings

"If you had to identify, in one word, the reason why the human race has not achieved, and never will achieve, its full potential, that word would be...meetings."
– comedian Dave Barry

Unfortunately, Dave Barry is right about meetings. In fact, a 2012 survey from *Industry Week* reports that people feel 30% of their time spent in meetings is *wasted.*

The thing is, time in meetings doesn't have to be wasted...it can be a valuable ROI if they're run right.

In fact, David called me several months later to catch me up on their progress. He had continued their weekly *Sellergy* (my version of synergy) meetings. He had also instituted my **Nine Guidelines for Well-Run Meetings** that are a joy for all involved.

---

1. Always have an agenda in front of everyone and stick to it.
2. Start on time and end on time. (No exceptions. Show that you mean what you say and you can be trusted to honor your time commitments.)
3. Only one person speaks at a time. No interrupting or talking over each other.
4. Each person speaks for a max of one to two minutes each time. No long, boring monologues.
5. Each person can only address a topic once—until it's clear everyone else who has something to say has his or her chance. (This prevents two people from dominating the conversation while everyone else sits on their hands.)
6. Each meeting starts off with each person sharing an up-to one minute of personal and/or professional "good news." This sets a positive tone and gives people something to look forward to instead of meetings just being about problems.
7. The goal is to find solutions—not fault. No finger pointing or blaming or shaming. The goal is to be proactive and focus on how to get better.

8. Each meeting features group brainstorming/strategizing of work challenges and generating crowd-sourced options that employees can use to improve results.
9. The meeting chair/host is rotated every week. Variety is the spice of "meetings." This is an excellent way to develop everyone's leadership, speaking, conflict resolution and facilitation skills.

This last guideline is a real favorite of mine. There's a predictability when the same person runs the meeting every time. Why not develop your employees by giving them an opportunity to be in charge of a weekly meeting? I have heard from many business owners who have been thrilled with the innovative, "Wouldn't have thought of that" approaches their employees initiated during their "week" as top dog.

Better yet, these ground rules create a "rising tide raising all boats *community*" where employees feel decisions are being made *by* them instead of *for* them. The resulting ownership gives them a sense of pride and commitment to quality that produces better morale and bottom line profits that benefit all involved.

If you've had the privilege of being part of a collaborative community, you've experienced what a pleasure it is to be surrounded by supportive people. You get to feed off their energy instead of having to supply all your own.

That is one of the reasons I prefer a group setting when it comes to yoga.

When I'm on the road working with clients, I discipline myself to practice yoga in my hotel room. After a long day sitting on planes or around tables, it's important to stretch my muscles, balance myself and breathe deeply. It centers me in what's important.

When I'm home however, I prefer to go to group yoga classes because there are so many different ways I benefit from being part of a community.

Some days, I may be a bit low on energy. When the alarm goes off in the morning for that 8 am class, I'm sorely tempted to turn over, pull the covers up and go back to sleep. Knowing my teacher and yoga buddies will be there, ready to greet me, is enough to get me out of bed and on my way.

Plus, there are certain poses I'm not comfortable doing on my own. Standing on my head just feels risky to me. I wouldn't think of attempting it without a supportive friend nearby, keeping me safe, looking out for me, having my front, my back and my neck.

Whether it's *Sellergy* in the work world or synergy in the yoga world; doing it together instead of alone makes it better.

Action Plan for Chapter 9

"I need people who push me to think differently so I can be the best me I can be."
– Michelle Obama

Has your company ever been in a sales slump? Do you sometimes get tired of going it alone? Do you have to figure out, on your own, how to handle challenges? Do you sometimes run low on energy and motivation?

What would it be like to bring everyone together and pool your intellectual resources? What would it be like to connect with colleagues on a personal as well as a professional basis?

Let's face it. Selling can be a lonely business.

We can feel vulnerable on our own without the support, encouragement and accountability our peers can provide. We put a ceiling on our development when we try to do everything on our own.

Sellergy meetings can create a much-welcomed caring community. They can also be used when a leader wants to improve group performance but doesn't have time to schedule a more formal sales training. It's actually implementing on the fly. *Sellergy* meetings generate exponential growth by capitalizing on the collective smarts of the group. It transforms selling from a solitary activity to a shared activity.

Sellergy meetings can focus on a specific challenge, such as how to ask for referrals or explain a rate increase. These sessions can be done whether you sell by phone or in person and have just one office or even multiple locations involved in *Sellergy* at the same time. When run well, they can eliminate feelings of isolation or of being overwhelmed. So, when are you scheduling your *Sellergy* meeting?

And, by the way, I am sometimes hired by companies to come in and conduct a one-day, intensive *Sellergy* meeting for their sales team.

I tailor each workshop according to the group's goals and needs, but here's what a sample schedule looks like:

One Day Intensive *Sellergy* Schedule:

8:00am - 8:15am	*Brief Introductions w/Good News*
8:15am -8:30am	*Brainstorming List of Launching Questions; Instructions on the Sellergy Approach*
8:30am - 10:00am	*Sell with Launching Question Focus* "How is your business changing?
10:00am - 10:30am	Debrief (report one success and one challenge) and a Break
10:30am - 12:00pm	*Sell with Launching Question Focus* "Under what circumstances would you consider a different provider?"

12:00pm - 1:00pm	Debrief (including role-plays) during a Working Lunch
1:00pm - 2:00 pm	*Sell with Launching Question Focus* Pick your own *Launching Question*
2:00pm - 2:30 pm	Debrief (report one success and one challenge) and a Break
2:30pm - 4:00 pm	*Sell with Launching Question Focus* Pick your own *Launching Question*
4:00pm - 4:30 pm	Debrief (report one success and one challenge) ; Prepare ongoing action plans and share best practices

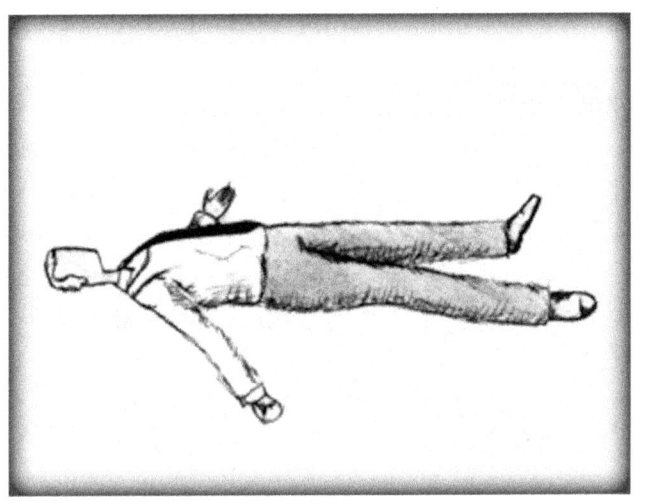

Chapter 10:
A = Appreciate and Celebrate

"I have found if you love life; life will love you back."

– Arthur Rubenstein

Next to Virksha-asana (Tree Pose), Shavasana (Corpse Pose) is my favorite yoga position.

If you haven't tried yoga before, you may be thinking Corpse Pose??

Work with me on this.

Corpse Pose is actually one of the most marvelously energizing, centering, relaxing, celebratory things you can do.

At the end of an intense yoga session, you can be pouring sweat. And you don't have to be in a hot yoga class to experience this. You can choose to participate in yoga in a mild way—or you can choose to participate in yoga in a wild way

I like to test myself, stretch myself and hold challenging poses until I'm on the brink of collapse. At the end of an hour of focused effort, it is sheer bliss to do the opposite of effort. Shavasana—Corpse Pose—is exactly what it sounds like. You get down on the ground, lie on your back with your arms at your sides and just *lie there.*

Aaahhh...bliss.

I remember the first yoga class I ever went to, thinking at the beginning that it wouldn't be much of a challenge and finishing in this very pose, so grateful for the reprieve. The purpose of Shavasana is to fully experience and appreciate your mind and body as they recover from being pushed to the edge.

This mindfulness serves a dual purpose:

1) We take stock of our accomplishments, congratulating ourselves for new flexibility, strength and stamina and appreciating the progress we have made that day.

2) We listen to what our body and mind are telling us about what to do next? Can we go to a deeper level of focus? Can we breathe more consistently, more rhythmically? Can we experience a sublime sense of centered calm?

Put Your Whole Soul Into It

"The whole road to happiness lies in two simple principles: find what interests you and that you do well—and put your whole soul into it, every bit of energy and natural ability you have." – John Rockefeller III

Rockefeller's quote articulates one of the reasons I love yoga. I am definitely interested in it and I put my whole soul into it and every bit of the natural ability and energy I can muster. Then to lie spent and revel in that intense experience is heartfelt happiness.

I have found that many of us are so busy—we have so many demands competing for our attention—we go through life perpetually preoccupied. To be 100% focused and engaged is rare. To tax our bodies and then lie quietly, awash in our feelings of reverence and gratitude, is a welcome contrast to our distracted, rush, rush lives.

It is through yoga—and through the resting pose of Shavasana—that I experienced this exquisite mindfulness. As a life-long salesman, I welcomed its many benefits and was amazed at the potential of carrying it outside the yoga studio.

Think about your sales history. How often do you reach a goal, only to immediately start thinking of your NEXT goal? Do you take time to appreciate and celebrate each achievement, or are you already on to your next client? When you complete a task, do you look back and see all the things you could have, should have, done better or faster? Are you your own worst critic? Do you tend to focus on what you do wrong instead of what you do well?

If you answered yes to any of the above questions, you'll probably appreciate a conversation I had with a psychologist friend of mine, Linda. In explaining what brings many people to a therapist's office, she told me this story:

"People come into my office because they're depressed, unhappy, going through a tough divorce, dealing with a health challenge, out of work, or having problems at work or with their relationships. But, all those 'problems' boil down to the same basic issue: things aren't going the way they want them to and it's causing them pain (sadness, anxiety, frustration, depression).

"The intensity of these emotions relates to how much is going wrong and how much effort my patients believe it will take to get things back on track. One of the first things we do is establish a 'baseline of functioning.'

"Though it can be difficult for patients to systematically take stock of everything that's going *wrong* in their life, what I'm looking for are those things that are still going *right*. For whatever reason, people sometimes lose the ability to accurately weigh the good and the bad in their life. In their mind, they are overwhelmed with the bad things, the failures, disappointments, grief and loss. They tend to overlook what is still working—they simply cannot remember it or make an emotional connection with what's right.

"In order for us to know if the therapy is working, I need to have a solid understanding of what my patient's life is like in that moment, so we know how to detect and measure change. This is essential in any situation, really. You cannot measure improvement or deterioration if you don't know the baseline of what you started with."

Linda is absolutely right. We all benefit from having a clear understanding of what is and what is not working. In order to make effective improvements, we need a way to measure our progress. Otherwise, we have no idea which of our efforts are helping and which are hurting.

Take Stock

"'Now' thyself is more important than 'know' thyself."
– Mel Brooks

In case you're wondering what this has to do with your sales efforts; what I've observed in my 20+ years as a consultant is that many of us are under so much pressure to produce, we drive, drive, drive, 24/7, nonstop…and never take a moment to give ourselves well-deserved pats on the back.

It was only after a particularly challenging yoga class that I realized the toll this takes. I was on a tight schedule that day, so needed to leave five minutes before the hour was up. I didn't even have time to shower or change; I just rushed home straight from class in order to make a Skype video call with a client.

The rest of that day, I felt "out-of-sorts." I had this vague feeling of "unfinished business." This dissatisfying feeling that something important was uncompleted nagged me all day. It wasn't until I went to bed that night that I had a chance to think back through the day and realize what was missing.

I had rushed right out of that yoga class. I hadn't had time to do Corpse Pose. I hadn't just "lain" there and let my heart rate, senses and breathing slow and settle. I hadn't reveled, relaxed, restored. I hadn't experienced those blissful moments when I was intensely, exquisitely alive, peaceful, and tranquil. Those precious few moments when all's right with the world.

That's when I promised myself I would never again rush out of a yoga class. If I needed to leave early for some reason, I would "complete the cycle" and do my own Corpse Pose so I honored the full circle experience.

Shavasana is a way of tending to our baseline. It is a time we schedule every day or week to take stock of how things are going. It is a time to identify efforts that have been fruitful or are showing promise; a time to let go of things that have proven ineffective. It is a time to acknowledge and appreciate our progress, give ourselves the encouragement that is oxygen to our soul...a time to reflect, revise and revel.

The longer we go without Shavasana, the longer we miss our life.

I read in the *Washington Post*, in an article by Kathleen Parker, that Steve Job's last words were supposedly, "Oh wow. Oh wow. Oh wow."

That is what Shavasana is. "Oh wow. Oh wow. Oh wow."

Imagine if that were your baseline. Imagine if your baseline belief is that life is a blessing and we're supposed to live in a state of gratitude, appreciation, and celebration. Imagine if your baseline belief is that, as a Sales Yogi, you:

- Appreciate your accomplishments.
- Embrace challenges as an opportunity to stretch and grow.
- Cultivate energy generated from successes and use that to fuel your progress.

Here are some questions to consider while you are in repose:

- How do I feel today? (Body and Mind)
- How does this feeling compare to last time?
- What efforts have I taken to initiate change?
- Based on how I'm feeling right now, is it working?
- How much longer am I prepared to try this before I move to the next option?
- What will it feel like (Body and Mind) when it's working?
- How will I measure improvement and how often will I take measurements?
- How will I reward improvement?

I recommend keeping some kind of record of your journey, be it blog, vlog, journal, scrapbook, pay stubs, client list or testimonials. There's certainly nothing wrong with being humble but there's quite a bit wrong with being blind to your own success.

Action Plan for Chapter 10

"When you are genuinely thrilled by someone else's success, that means you are right on the track of your own." – Esther Hicks

When you lie down tonight, practice Shavasana.

Breathe deeply, in and out through your nose and take stock of all that you have accomplished, today, this week, this month, this year.

Reflect on your successes and contributions.

Revel in those achievements and contributions. Follow Esther Hicks' advice—be thrilled for others' success *and* your own!

If you can record these accomplishments in some way, it will benefit you on those days when you struggle to remember your strengths. We all do, sometimes. Just remember to be a friend to yourself instead of your own worst critic.

Next, plan for your future. What is your intent for tomorrow, this week?

Chose a priority goal and envision how you plan to achieve it.

Having an endpoint in mind is beneficial, knowing what it looks like when you are on the right track, is even better.

To plan your short-term goals, ask yourself these questions.

---

1. What is my intent—my primary goal—for tomorrow?
2. How do I plan to achieve my goal tomorrow? What steps will I take to ensure it happens?
3. How will I know when my intent, my goal, happens? What will it look like?
4. What is my intent—my primary goal—for this week? What steps am I going to take to ensure this gets done?
5. How will I know when my intent, my goal, happens? What will it look like?

For example, a client of mine does a little victory dance every time she reaches her daily and weekly sales goal. She always makes her intent and goals measurable, whether it's getting one new solid lead, closing a deal of a minimum of $1000, or making three warm calls that result in follow-up meetings. When she hits her goal, she gets up in her office and does her little happy dance. It's her way of celebrating her success.

How can you make Shavasana a daily part of your personal and professional life? You will notice dramatic improvement in your performance, productivity and peace of mind when you do. The self-awareness and appreciation that comes from practicing mindfulness will enrich your relationships and results. Perhaps most importantly, your "Oh wow, Oh wow, Oh wow" baseline mentality will keep you centered in your Sales Yogi mentality.

Section 3:

What Other *Sales Yoga* Principles

Can I Integrate into

My Practice?

"To exist is to change,
To change is to mature,
To mature is to go on creating oneself endlessly."

– Henri Bergson

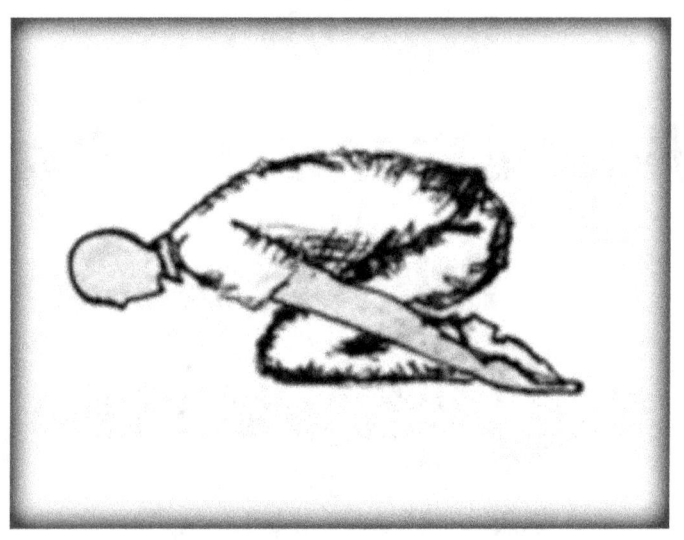

Chapter 11:
Keep Your Totems Top of Mind

"'The horror of that moment,' the King went on,
'I shall never forget!'
'You will, though,' the Queen said, 'if you don't
make a memorandum of it.'"

– Lewis Carroll, Alice in Wonderland

Early in my career, I was a "headhunter."

I worked in one of those open-floor offices with desks clustered around the room. In an attempt to give our spaces a little personality, my colleagues and I brought in personal items and decorated our desks and walls with pictures of family and friends, plants and meaningful items so it became our professional little "home."

When I was in serious need of a break, I would grab a cup of coffee and wander around the floor perimeter, checking in with my colleagues.

One co-worker, Manny, had covered his area with post-its, mini-posters and family photos. He had also put up shelves that held a virtual bazaar of intriguing trinkets. One day, my curiosity won out and I trekked over and asked him about his treasure.

"Manny, what on earth is all this stuff?"

He laughed, shrugged his shoulders, and with a sheepish expression on his face said, "They're just reminders of things I want, things I'm striving for, things I care about, you know."

I nodded my head like I understood and kept scanning his shelves. Something in particular caught my eye, a mini-hourglass with the bulbs painted so you couldn't see how much sand was in it.

I imagined it had some metaphorical meaning for Manny, something to do with the fact that we never really know how much time we have left or some deep symbolism like that. I asked Manny to explain the mysterious object, "Manny, what about that one? What is that supposed to remind you of?"

Manny picked up the hourglass, and turned it over in his hands a few times. He rubbed the smooth glass with his thumbs and hummed to himself for a moment. I was sure he was recalling some words of wisdom offered to him by a mentor or a memory of a lesson hard-learned.

Then, Manny began to chuckle. He turned to me and said with a wide grin, "You know what, Scott?"

"What?" I replied.

"I don't remember!"

How Can We Remember our Good Intentions?

"I have a photographic memory. I just haven't developed it yet." – comedian Henny Youngman

Manny was so overloaded with things to remember, he needed reminders for his reminders. And Manny's not alone.

As individuals living in the information age, we're suffering from what my author friend, Sam Horn, calls "InfoBesity." We have way too much information to process, remember and apply on a day-to-day basis.

We have passwords, pin numbers, phone numbers, door codes, shopping lists, client lists, parking spot assignments, birthdays, anniversaries and most importantly, how to work your new Smartphone. And, this list barely scratches the surface.

While I'm sure there's an app (or 50) to remember all that for us, we need to distill what's crucial and keep it top of mind as our performance depends on our ability to recall and do what's *most* important to executing our jobs efficiently and effectively.

The way to do that is to keep what's vital IN-SIGHT, IN-MIND.

Remember my client who put her "YET" on her refrigerator, notebook and iPad covers? She knew that, despite her best intentions, her commitment to "create a not yet" would get drowned out in the day's InfoBesity unless she kept that word in front of her.

The good news is, you can counteract InfoBesity and improve your memory with *cues*. Memory cues are physical, visual or auditory triggers that help you remember things you would otherwise forget when you're inundated with to-dos.

Stay Centered in Who You Are and How You Want to Show Up

"To be yourself in a world that, day and night, is trying to turn you into someone else, is the hardest battle you will ever fight and keep fighting." – e.e. cummings

So, what does this have to do with sales? As you've grown and honed your skills over the course of your career, you've accumulated best practices, lessons-learned and nuggets of advice. These pearls of wisdom are those aha's, thought-provoking quotes, or acronyms that resonate and that help you maintain clarity, motivation and determination.

Remembering and applying those nuggets can be the difference between meeting or missing a quota, closing or losing a contract, earning a well-deserved promotion...or not.

That's why it's important to create your own "totems" and memory cues. A "totem" is defined as "anything serving as a distinctive, venerated emblem or symbol." And, in case you're wondering, "venerated" means "to treat or regard with reverence."

In your rush, rush world, it's important to keep meaningful totems and cues that remind you of who you want to be, of how you want to show up.

Instead of allowing your lessons-learned and best intentions to disappear and be out-of-sight, out-of-mind, post or place them where you will see them throughout the day. Then, if someone is rude to you and you're about to lash back, you can glance at them, calm yourself down and regain and retain your Sales Yogi mentality.

If you have a frustrating day and no one seems interested in buying, you can look at your letters from satisfied customers and ground yourself in the fact that your work does matter and that you DO make a difference and this is just one of those days.

The key is, don't do it like Manny. You gain nothing by flooding yourself with so many reminders that you can't recall their purpose. Keep your list to seven best practice tips, or seven inspiring quotes, or seven goals you want to remember, or seven best-practices you want to integrate and implement into your daily sales interactions.

Memory experts say we can only keep seven bits of information in our "working memory"...which is information that we can access and use when needed, in the moment.

In a yoga class, the best teachers offer just a few instructions or insights during each pose. This allows the students to stay centered in their practice instead of being distracted by too many details. The practice of *Sales Yoga* is built on the idea of being open and focused instead of overwhelmed and frazzled.

Don't add to the InfoBesity by surrounding yourself with too many totems or cues. Our goal is to inspire ourselves to stay centered so we act in alignment with our values and goals... not to become so overwhelmed we become intimidated and immobilized.

So, what meaningful totem could you keep in your cubicle or by your desk so it keeps you mindful of how and who you want to be? Take it into your office tomorrow and put it where you will see it throughout the day so you remember what matters.

Action Plan for Chapter 11

"There are three things I can't remember; names, keys ... and I can't remember the third thing."
– coffee mug slogan

Below are some examples of totems and memory cues you can use to stay centered in being the quality of salesperson you want to be. Make sure to keep these items in-sight, in-mind so you keep them top of mind.

Memory Totems

Physical	Visual	Auditory
• A bracelet with a charm on it that says "Listen" to remind yourself to practice *HalfTalk* and *Mind Over Mouth*	• A post-it on your computer monitor showing the word "Shield" with a circle around it and a line through it.	• A mantra like "Buyers see me as a trusted peer" you repeat to yourself before every sales conversation.
• A mini-sculpture of a person doing Tree Pose on your shelf to remind you to stay balanced	• A watch you gave yourself as a reward for *HalfTalk* points won in your *Mind Over Mouth* game.	• An acronym like ABC = Always Be Collaborating
• Set your phone alarm to vibrate a few minutes before your meeting is supposed to end so you know when to wrap it up and respect your buyer's time limits.	• A sign on your door that says "As a Sales Yogi, I create win-win relationships with everyone I meet."	• A song you play on your way to a meeting that pumps you up and motivates you to walk in with confidence and positive energy.

Chapter 12:
Manage Your Moods with Mantras

*"I've been on an emotional roller coaster recently.
The other day my mood ring exploded."*

– comedian Janine DiTullio

Goggle defines "Mantra" as: *A word or sound repeated to aid in concentration in meditation; a statement that is frequently repeated; a characteristic formula or refrain.*

A mantra is an auditory memory trigger meant to express a great deal of meaning in a relatively short period of time. Mantras aren't just important for the words by which they are comprised; they also serve as a representation (memory chain) of a desired emotion, state of mind, achievement or measure of caution. In sales, a positive state of mind is a requirement for sustainable success.

As we repeat a mantra, over and over again, we allow ourselves to become familiar with that concept. Over time that familiarity becomes comforting and grounding, which strengthens our resolve and improves our performance in any given task. In the beginning, we may resist the idea by:

- Coming up with reasons why it won't work
- Feeling silly for having attempted it at all
- "Forgetting" to practice the mantra
- Deciding we don't have time to attend to the mantra

These are all perfectly normal responses. Our minds and bodies are efficient machines and prefer not to take up new activities, skills or mindsets unless there is a guaranteed reward. We generate resistance as a test to see whether or not our new efforts are worth the resources.

There's no need to add to the resistance by getting frustrated or irritated with our lack of progress. A mantra is not a forceful process. Like water over a stone, eventually it will cut a path through even the densest rock. That is the power of a mantra: to slowly wash away our rough edges rather than attempt to pound them out of existence.

Whether it is "Say little, ask a lot" or the Serenity Prayer or something of your own creation, your mantra will be effective if it meets the criteria below.

- **Concise:** While it can be tempting to have a running conversation with ourselves, we can often get distracted by our internal monologue. Keep that peanut gallery under control by giving it something to focus on.
- **Clear:** Choosing something straight forward allows you to split your attention between your mantra and what's going on around you. Something more poetic and complex may hold a great deal of meaning and sound beautiful and may also pull your attention inward and away from your buyer.
- **Repeatable:** If you're particularly distracted, sometimes repeating your mantra out loud can harness your scattered thoughts. This means your mantra is best as something

easy to say over and over rather than a tongue twister or something too long to remember.

- **Positive:** Rather than saying "I don't do this" (such as, "I don't talk too much") identify the alternative behavior, thought, or feeling and say "I do/feel/think" ("I talk less and less every day"). By giving yourself a positive command, you automatically fill the gap left by the behavior/thought/feeling you are trying to stop.
- **Rhythmic**, rhyming and/or lyrical (bonus points for this one): A simple rhyme, poem or song lyrics that inspire, encourage and are jam-packed with emotional content can bolster your courage when the going gets tough.

Here's one from Tim Duncan that meets all the criteria and was repeated by Jeff Goldblum's character, Ricky Hayman in the 1998 movie *Holy Man:*

Good, Better, Best
Never Let it Rest,
'Til Your Good is Better
And Your Better is Best

I have a mantra I say to myself on my yoga mat while I'm waiting for each class to begin. I breathe in for four counts while thinking "Receive...." and breathe out for four counts while saying to myself, "Breathe...."

Inhale four counts with "Receive...." Exhale four counts with "Breathe...."

In as little as two minutes, I have regulated my breathing and quieted my mind. No thinking about the rush hour traffic on the way to the studio. No thinking about needing to catch a plane in the morning. No thinking about the PowerPoint slides I need to prepare for my presentation.

In four counts with "Receive...." Out for four counts with "Breathe...."

Try it. Don't you already feel more peaceful? Less stressed?

Action Plan for Chapter 12

*"The word 'meditation' is rather an abused word ...
it would be much better to use the word 'quiet time;'
in which a person shuts out the noise of the world
and enters into himself." – Bishop Fulton Sheen*

If the idea of a mantra appeals to you, take some time after reading this chapter to develop one of your own. Check it against the criteria above and then start implementing your mantra in your sales approach. You may want to generate more than one option in case the first one you try doesn't feel right.

I like the Goldilocks (from the old "Goldilocks and the 3 Bears" story) approach to trying out a new skill. If you generate three options, you will likely find that one is not enough of something, one is too much of another and the third will be just right.

Remember that one of the many benefits of selecting a meaningful mantra is that it focuses you on an emotion you want to feel and a characteristic you want to project. If you're walking into a high-pressure sales meeting; go the bathroom beforehand and give yourself five minutes to "go into yourself." Silently repeat with each inhalation and exhalation "Calm and Confident" or "I love my job" or "Think win-win" or "Listen, Listen" to center yourself in a Sales Yogi mentality that will serve you and your client.

Once you've selected your sales mantra, remember it takes at least 18 days to form a habit so give yourself a month of practicing it in the morning, before important meetings and before you go to sleep. Fill your mind with your mantra so it becomes second nature and these qualities are part of who you are and how you feel.

Chapter 13:
Sell With Integrity

"The supreme quality for leadership is unquestionable integrity. Without it, no real success is possible."

– former president Dwight D. Eisenhower

Since the word "slick" is often used to describe a salesperson, I looked it up.

Webster's Dictionary defines "slick" as: *smooth in manners, suave, shrewdly adroit, ingenious, cleverly devised, slippery, deftly executed, polished but superficial.*

I realized that out of all the words in that definition, most people would probably think of the last one when thinking of salespeople: polished but superficial.

None of them are complimentary. Unfortunately, many salespeople are seen as having a hidden agenda, out for their own benefit, manipulative, untrustworthy and to be approached with caution if not completely avoided. I'm on a mission to reverse this negative stereotype, especially after this experience below.

Early in my career, I paid several thousand dollars to attend a weekend workshop in Marin County, CA with two big-name sales "gurus" who promised to share their "trade secrets" on how to grow a profitable sales business.

Like many of the 200 attendees there, I was excited to hear the best practices from these sales icons. At 7:55 am, I had my coffee in one hand, note pad in the other, and made my way to the front row to be as close as possible to the "action."

An hour into the program, I started to get a bit nervous. They hadn't said anything profound or insightful. The whole reason I'd taken off time from work, flown across the country, and paid all that money was to expand my knowledge base. So far, everything they'd shared was obvious and, frankly, obnoxious. They were promoting the same old slimy and slippery sales methods I'd heard before.

By lunch a number of us were feeling ripped off. The entire morning had consisted pretty much of these two telling stories. They kept promising to get to the meat of the program, the specific "how-to's," but it never happened.

We were three hours into a six-hour workshop and, contrary to their advertising, this was Smarmy Sales 101. Still, I'm an optimistic guy and wasn't quite ready to give up so I headed back in to the hotel ballroom after lunch and settled in for round two.

Things didn't get better; in fact, they got worse. The stories and "tips" now centered on even more misleading, manipulative tactics designed to separate people from their wallets. I kept thinking to myself, "This is exactly why the public thinks so poorly of us."

By the 2:30 pm break, I was done. Their marketing brochure promised a money back guarantee if you were dissatisfied for *any* reason. I was dissatisfied for *many* reasons, so I headed to the registration table and politely asked the staffer for a refund.

He was gob-smacked. Apparently, if I read his expression correctly, no one had ever asked for their money back. Guess what he did next? If you guessed that he tried the same slick sales tactics the "gurus" were sharing from the stage in an effort to change my mind, you're right.

"That's too bad you're unhappy with the program. Perhaps you'd like a copy of our video series so you have more time to absorb and process the material."

"No thanks," I replied, recognizing that he'd just implied I was unhappy because I couldn't *understand* the material. "I'd just like my money back."

"I'm surprised you want a refund. These experts are universally respected as the best in their field and they always get excellent evaluations. Perhaps you'd like a free consult with one of our certified trainers so he could answer any questions you have?"

"No, thanks. I simply want a refund as is promised in your literature."

Eventually the staffer gave in and rather begrudgingly gave me a full credit on my credit card. I spent the rest of the day walking through the redwoods and thinking about why I was so disappointed with my experience. I was particularly annoyed with the staffer's implication that my dissatisfaction was somehow my fault.

I realized, "This is how many people feel after an unsatisfactory experience with a salesperson. They feel mislead, manipulated, taken advantage of, resentful. The word that comes closest to how I felt was…yucky.

As a result of that experience, I resolved to sell with integrity. This was before I discovered yoga, but even back then I was clear I did NOT want to do to others what was done to me that weekend. I was going to set an example of integrity so my customers could always trust that I was acting with their best interests in mind.

Leo Tolstoy said, "Everyone thinks of changing the world, no one thinks of changing himself." We may not be able to change the world; we may not be able to change the entire sales profession, we *can* change ourselves. We can commit to creating win-win relationships where everyone involved feels they've received value.

Action Plan for Chapter 13

*"You follow your ethics for inner reasons, not
because someone is keeping score
or because you will be punished if you don't."*
– Jon Kabat-Zinn

The next time someone is selling to you, take a moment to consider how their approach makes you feel.

- Do you feel rushed, coerced, induced or convinced?
- Does the salesperson give you the impression that you will be missing out if you don't take advantage of this great deal?
- Do you feel like you're being talked into something you don't want or need?
- Does the salesperson imply that you're using poor judgment if you don't agree?
- When you say yes or no, does the salesperson jump right in to up-sell you or sell you something else that really isn't much better than the first option?
- Does it seem like s/he cares more about closing a deal than meeting your needs or solving a problem?

Paying attention to these experiences will give you some insight into how it feels to be the recipient of heavy-handed, high-pressure, unethical sales techniques.

Make the commitment to be dramatically different. Tell yourself, "The yuck stops here."

May Sarton said, "One must think like a hero to behave like a decent human being." Resolve to act in integrity and sell with integrity. The way to be a hero to your customers is simply to act like a decent human being and to treat everyone with the dignity they want, need and deserve.

Chapter 14:
Give Your Brain and Your Buyer Homework

"I used to think the human brain was the most fascinating part of the body, and then I thought, 'What is telling me that?'"

– comedian Emo Phillips

Do you have days where your brain doesn't seem to work very well?

The good news is, you can prompt your brain—and your buyer's brain—to get to work so you're both mentally engaged instead of mentally absent.

I firmly believe in giving the buyer homework. I know what you're thinking. Most times I can barely get a prospective client to listen to me at all. How am I going to get them to listen *and* agree to a homework assignment?

You're right! It can be difficult to build this kind of relationship, which is why we fall back on the *Sales Yoga* premise: Everything is about the buyer. When we generate homework, each question, task or thought assignment is geared toward benefiting the client and their business. People are much more likely to engage in the process when they can see the obvious benefit for themselves in completing the task.

We rarely close a deal in the first conversation, which means there will be some downtime between our initial conversation, negotiation and closing. More often than not, these gaps in inter-action are the times when doubts arise, concerns develop or peo-ple simply forget to think about you at all.

Clients jump on the internet to do some research, recall con-versations they've had with our competitors and start to compare notes and talk to friends and colleagues about what you've put on the table thus far.

It's important for us to shape that downtime, as much as we can, into something that benefits the buyer, our selling process, and the relationship. There are things we can do during the sales conversation as well as crafting homework assignments that fol-low our clients out the door or off the phone.

A few years ago, I was working with Melody, Chief Financial Officer (CFO) of a multi-site global tech company. Our con-versations were primarily over the phone in preparation for a meeting where the finalized proposal would be reviewed and blessed, or not. She and I had been working together on this as a multi-stage operation because we didn't have all the decision makers at the same site or even in the same country. I knew I needed her buy-in or I'd never get to talk with the other people with power.

Melody was well informed and attentive to the needs of her company so I knew she would be a solid source of information. I decided to give Melody homework in order to keep me and my company top of mind, while also continuing my information gathering.

Her first piece of homework was to think about what objec-tives they would want to accomplish if we were to work together.

This particular homework assignment benefited both of us in four ways:

---

1. Melody would be well prepared when we had our next meeting.
2. Even if Melody had other providers pitching to her, she would be thinking most specifically about me.
3. My homework assignment was about visualizing a positive, successful working relationship together, encouraging her to think of me and my company in a positive light.
4. Melody would come back to our meeting with specific needs and goals so I could individualize solutions in a way my competitors would not.

The next meeting, by telephone, involved Melody and the other decision makers. I gave similar homework, encouraging them to really delve into and develop their idea of the value they would receive once we accomplished the objectives.

My final homework assignment before the "big meeting" where we would discuss my proposal was quite simple and really helped me close the deal. I asked the leaders to think about everything we'd come up with up until that point and consider anything we might have missed, anything else I needed to know.

Again, this task benefited both of us:

---

1. In thinking of anything we'd missed, they were essentially helping me generate my list of potential objections to my proposal.
2. Encouraging them to review our discussions to date would prompt them to think about me a little more before our final meeting and in a slightly different way.

3. Asking for what we had missed would also prompt them to mentally review our relationship thus far, remembering our positive interaction and sense of being understood.

It's a relatively passive process for me and very similar to the homework assignments given at the end of a yoga class. After completing an invigorating session, yoga teachers often ask their students to recall the positive feelings and calming energy they experience during class and carry that through everything they do that day and for the rest of the week. This prompts students to think about yoga, its concepts, premises and goals, even when they are out of class, and supports their continued progress.

When you practice *Sales Yoga*, giving homework to your clients allows them to continue to experience the benefit of remembering you and remembering your service and value. There is mindfulness in this selling process and mindfulness in yoga. When you are thinking about your client and their needs, and they are thinking about you and your value, we call this Mutual Mindfulness and it is the best form of a sales relationship.

- How would you like your clients to think of you when you're not in the room?
- Instead of leaving clients to their own devices, what would it be like to guide their thoughts back to you through a homework assignment?
- How might you and your client benefit from Mutual Mindfulness?

Action Plan for Chapter 14

"Anyone who stops learning is old, whether at twenty or eighty. Anyone who keeps learning is young." – Henry Ford

The next time you are doing a multi-stage sales process; consider some homework questions for your client that benefit both of you. Here is one thing you can do during the conversation that sets up a great homework assignment:

When you sell, you want to make sure there are always multiple options on the table. The last thing you want to do is come across to the buyer as an all-or-nothing salesperson. That benefits no one. Providing multiple, tiered options with varying prices and values allows you some flexibility with the buyer. It also gives them some power and comfort in selecting the option that is best for them.

Rather than pulling for a yes or no answer ("Yes, I'll buy" or "No thanks"), it's a multiple choice question where no is significantly outnumbered by yes's of all shapes and sizes. Options one, two and three all scale in price as well as the amount of value that is delivered.

Now your clients go home with three options to consider. Their homework becomes making the decision between the three options, ensuring that they're thinking and talking about you until the next meeting.

Here is a review of the assignments and questions for clients mentioned above, as well as a few other options:

- What are the objectives and goals of our relationship, if we were to work together?
- How would you like to see your business improve through our interaction? How would you measure that improvement?

- What are you hoping my company can provide that no one else has been able to deliver?
- What products/services would you like to see adapted to meet your company's specific needs?
- Now that we've developed a solid proposal, what, if anything, have we missed?
- What else should I know about you? Your company? What else would you like to learn about this opportunity that would help make this relationship a win-win?

Chapter 15:
Remember That Practice
Makes Profit

"You play the way you practice."

– Football coach Pop Warner

I've never agreed with the saying, "Practice makes perfect." Nothing is ever perfect...so that saying doesn't make sense.

Practice is an opportunity to get better, to get as good as we can possibly be. Practice helps us figure out what doesn't work. Practice helps us "get in a groove" so we can think on our feet (and seat) when something unexpected happens. Practice gives us a baseline of skills so we can get creative and spontaneously generate options in the moment.

In my first sales job, I was an executive search consultant, a.k.a. headhunter. The job itself, being a matchmaker for great companies and people, gave me great pleasure, while the learning environment taught me how to improve myself, both as a professional and an individual.

We used to sit in a big open room with a dozen employees. There were no walls, nothing to block or diminish our interaction while working. This open floor allowed us to listen to one another, learn from each other and provide feedback when requested.

Each Friday, we would all turn our chairs in and gather for a structured practice session. I spearheaded the session because I found it so beneficial and wanted to be involved as much as possible. The major focus was overcoming objections and rather than attempt perfect practice, we aimed for worst-case scenario practice. Our goal was to make the role play much harder than it would ever really be with an actual buyer.

Depending on the occasion, the "buyer" was either a company who was hiring talent or a person open to (buying into) a new job. We picked different objections like:

- "Your fee is too high."
- "We're already working with another agency."
- "I don't want to go to that part of town."
- "I've heard bad things about that company."

We would take these different objections and practice them with one another. One person would play the client or the candidate while the other would play the recruiter, the executive search consultant. The candidate would push and push, resist and resist, while the recruiter did their best to generate plausible questions and responses to the objections. Meanwhile, the other ten people in the group would offer feedback, suggestions and ideas as the role-play went on.

While this was pretty anxiety provoking for the recruiter, he or she learned a great deal about how to operate under pressure and think and respond nimbly. The crowd got a third-person perspective on how these conversations could evolve and what our responses may sound like to the buyer. Our goal was to get rid of the stuttering, emotional reactions, and dead-end responses while expanding our ability to cope with a particularly difficult situation.

After our Friday practice, each of us left work better prepared for that stressful situation while also gaining perspective and appreciation for our less challenging interactions. The practice session wasn't meant to be perfect. In fact, it was our time to get all of our potential mistakes out in the open for feedback and correction. We could all agree that making mistakes in the practice session was much better than making them during a sales conversation.

However, what we also learned was how to think on our feet. Rarely did we actually use the exact phrasing or encounter the exact scenario experienced during our Friday sessions. What became familiar was that sense of adaptation and rather than being scared or leery of uncharted territory, we had gained confidence in our ability to color outside the lines.

One of the biggest problems in the sales industry is that, while we are all willing to learn new techniques, we are afraid to use them. And, more often than not, the first time you get to use a new technique is with a live audience and, if it doesn't go well, it could cost you the deal.

We don't want to fail and look like a fool. In our Friday session, that pressure was gone. There was no risk being taken; nothing to lose. The only pressure was getting up in front of our colleagues and making the inevitable mistakes. The multifold benefits outweighed the ego blow:

- **Practice makes profit:** Every week we all got a little bit better rather than sitting at our desks, in our own little worlds, stagnating.
- **Trying new things:** After everyone accepted that mistakes were welcome, the pressure of perfection faded.

- **No one was ever as hard on us as we were on ourselves:** Our over-the-top structured sessions made working with our customers much easier.

Now, to shift this from a hard-selling technique to a *Sales Yoga* technique is very simple. Instead of trying to come up with smooth responses, convincing statements, counter-statistics or counter offers, the salesperson uses questions to better understand the buyer's concerns, evoke solutions, and gain agreement for a resolution that removes or eliminates the objection. Since the buyer is an equal partner in either solving their own issue or collaborating with you on a solution, no heavy-handed convincing or inducing is necessary.

How do you do this? Our action plan for this chapter shows you how.

Before we do, I couldn't wrap up this chapter on "practice" without talking about my appreciation for why they call it a yoga "practice." For years, I could not do a "fold," a pose where you grab your feet…without bending your knees. Some very limber people, (i.e., dancers, divers and gymnasts in particular), can do this without even thinking about it.

Not me. For years, we're talking *years* here, it seemed like the impossible dream. I thought I was just going to have to accept it was something I could *not* do.

That's where practice comes in. Instead of giving up and quitting, I just kept practicing. And practicing. And one day, instead of just getting close, I was able to grab my feet…without bending (or buckling) my knees. Hallelujah.

So, as you use these techniques, if they don't work immediately, or even after weeks of practice…don't give up, don't quit. Keep practicing your *Sales Yoga*. The only way to fail is to stop trying.

Action Plan for Chapter 15

"When I am right, no one remembers; when I am wrong, no one forgets." – baseball umpire Doug Harvey

One of the purposes of practice is to identify what's going wrong...and correct it; and to identify what's going right...and compliment it and continue it.

Here are some examples of objections with traditional sales (TS) responses and their alternative *Sales Yoga* (SY) questions. Our goal is to shift away from the instinctual response to argue or convince the buyer (wrong) and shift towards a more collaborative, respectful conversation (right).

As we've already clarified, the key is to respond in the form of a question.

- *"Your price is too high."*

(TS): "How about if we lower the price for the first year and offer you our complimentary consultation service at no extra cost."

(SY): "What would make it worth paying our price?"

- *"We're already working with another vendor."*

(TS): "And if you'd just change over to us, we could give you the same services for 5% less."

(SY): "Under what circumstances would you consider a different vendor?"

- *"I've heard negative things about your company."*

(TS): "I can assure you those are just rumors from our competitors. Our company has an excellent reputation and a long history of exemplary customer service."

(SY): "What specifically have you heard? How can I demonstrate that those issues are inaccurate?

Our goal is to keep the line of communication open. It can be tempting to argue with something you disagree with or immediately try to sooth concerns. However, your potential buyers expect you to argue or contradict them so they'll be on the defensive as soon as they hear you make any attempts to counter their objection.

Rather than jump down their throat in an attempt to correct their "wrong thinking," ask a question to find the source of the issue. The last thing you want to do is jump right in to a solution, only to have them come back and tell you that it does not address their concerns. This taking a "stab in the dark" approach rarely, if ever, works.

The next time someone objects to your suggestion or offer, in your personal or professional life, take a moment to ask some questions about where the objection is coming from. Be sure to keep your questions neutral and open-ended (using *Launching Questions* as often as possible) so the other person feels heard, unjudged and unpressured. Your questions will benefit no one if they are rhetorical, sarcastic or leading.

When you practice, whether your focus is on objections or other areas of the sales process, pay attention to how people respond. Do they strike up a conversation, avoid your question or get frustrated and stop talking? These are clues to how your style of questions has made them feel. The more neutral and exploratory you can be the better. Remember, practice makes profit IF you do it right.

Chapter 16:
Strive For Excellence,
Not Perfection

"I don't use the word perfect because nothing's ever perfect. I strive for excellence."

– Barbra Streisand

Have you ever noticed that the professions called "practices" are the ones where lives and health hang in the balance?

Internists, chiropractors, veterinarians, psychologists and psychiatrists all have "practices" even though they all have Certifications, Masters and Doctoral Degrees declaring them experts in their respective fields.

I asked Michael, a friend of mine who is an internist (a medical doctor), why they call it a "practice." He said, "Well Scott, we call it a *practice* because we acknowledge that, while we are experts, we don't know everything there is to know about what we do. I *practice* medicine but I will never perfect it.

"I imagine it makes people uncomfortable to think of their doctors as practicing on them."

"Actually, it should. So many people go to doctors and feel as if they are at the mercy of the doctor's ability. Few people actually go to a doctor and interview them as if they employed the doctor, which they actually do.

"Could you imagine going in to a doctor's office and asking for credentials, breadth of experience and references? I bet we'd all be frozen in shock! Doctors are employed by their patients just as much as they are employed by the hospital or clinic. If the patients stopped coming, there would be no hospital, no clinic, and no business.

"One thing that is true of all these people who practice a profession is that all have continuing education requirements in order to stay licensed and keep *practicing*. That means each of us acknowledges that we will not be practicing the same techniques in five years that we do today. Just like few of us are practicing exactly what we learned when we had just graduated from med school.

"Actually, continuing to practice the same techniques or approaches when something has been scientifically proven to work better is against our ethical code and could cost us our license. Maybe more people should practice their professions rather than run around thinking they've mastered their trade. Maybe more people would be willing to keep learning rather than get stuck in the same old routine.

"One thing I can guarantee you is, those doctors, psychiatrists or whatever, that truly believe they are practitioners and not masters will be the best at what they do. Someone who is willing to keep learning is always going to be better than the one who has decided they know it all, in the long run."

Michael has a great point, especially when he states that more people should think of themselves as practitioners rather than masters. How much more accepting would work environments be if we thought of ourselves as forever practicing?

Our ultimate goal is to advance. Perfection is in advancement. As long as we are moving forward we are practicing, perfectly. Yoga holds a very similar structure.

Yogi is defined as: a yoga practitioner. Not an expert or a guru. Someone who is practicing yoga, working on advancing their abilities.

I am a Sales Yogi, a practitioner of *Sales Yoga* and while I may have mastered many of these techniques, I am aware that there is still much work to be done. There are times when I catch myself talking too much, making statements instead of asking questions. I've had moments where someone has come up with an objection that didn't make any sense to me and I was so tempted to point out the flawed logic.

As a Sales Yogi I acknowledge the misstep, remind myself of my goals and try again. Like a baseball player, my goal is to improve my batting average every chance I get but no one ever bats 1.000 and no one expects them too. Actually, a great hitter is still expected to fail more times than he or she succeeds. We can expect more of ourselves in sales but the concept is still sound.

When approaching your own work, think of yourself as a sales practitioner, someone who has mastered their craft and is constantly looking for continuing education, advancements in technique and enhancements in approach.

There is no sense in continuing to use arcane methods that no longer apply to our information-inundated culture. These techniques were developed during a time when people lived in smaller communities, when they already knew who they were buying from.

Anne Lamott said "Expectations are resentments under construction." When we expect a standard for ourselves that is both implausible and unsatisfying we set ourselves up for bitterness, burnout and boredom. Learning is stimulating, interesting and challenging; three things we need to stay at the top of our game in our chosen profession.

Often salespeople think of themselves as masters and include with that title the idea that they know everything there is to know, and will never need to change their approach. Such an expectation repels them from learning and ultimately leads to the feeling that their job is no longer challenging enough. While the solution to such a feeling is simple, the change in mindset can be very difficult.

Acknowledging that there is something more to learn can be humbling. The mindset of "ultimate mastery" is counterproductive in the long term. However, it can be deceptively soothing in the short term for relieving anxiety related to challenges from peers or supervisors or recent failure. Thinking of ourselves as at the top of our game allows us the ability to dismiss the opinions and observations of others.

If we think of ourselves as knowing everything, we can interpret critiques as coming from people who are "less experienced" or "not as talented" as we are, or that they simply "don't know what they're talking about." It's easy to dismiss things we don't want to hear when we decide that the people giving us the unwanted information are somehow unqualified. Rather than see the situation as a learning opportunity, we close our ears and take comfort in our expertise.

Action Plan for Chapter 16

*"My friend thought he'd never get a date.
I told him to 'Think positive.' Now he's positive
he's never going to get a date."
– comedian Brother Sammy Shore*

If you find yourself struggling to accept suggestions, feedback or constructive critique this may be because your evaluation of your skills is too rigid. You can prepare yourself on your own for uncomfortable feedback by exploring your skill set as well as areas in which you need improvement.

Being aware of the areas in which you'd like to improve can make hearing such feedback less jarring. People tend to resist critique when we receive negative feedback on a skill or project we feel is strong or went well. By expanding our thought process beyond "good" and "bad," toward something more grayscale, we can more easily accept, absorb or dismiss criticism.

Rigid: Here's how people tend to see their skill set. It's a black and white, all or nothing list of skills you either have or don't have. This leaves little way to measure progress objectively:

I'm Good at:	I'm Bad at:
Selling to Individuals	Selling to Groups
Cold Calls to Small Businesses	Cold Calls to Large Businesses
Overcoming Objections about Price	Overcoming Objections about Service
Asking Questions	Remembering my Mantra

Flexible: Here's a different way of measuring your progress. Rather than deciding if you've "got it" or not, rate your skills on a scale of 1 to 10. Rating the skill at a 1 means you either have no practice with the skill or haven't tried to implement it yet. Rating a skill at a 10 mean you have mastery over that skill and, much more often than not, are able to utilize it with success.

Skill	Rating 1 (No Skill) - 10 (Mastery)
Selling to Individuals	9
Selling to Groups	3
Cold Calls to Small Businesses	7
Cold Calls to Large Businesses	2
Overcoming Objections about Price	8
Overcoming Objections about Service	4
Asking Questions	6
Remembering my Mantra	5

By measuring your progress in this way, you can strive to make incremental improvements. For example, by practicing, as in the previous chapter, cold calls to large businesses, your score, after just a few sessions of practice, could climb from a 2 to a 4. Now that's tangible progress!

Chapter 17:
Shape Your Sales Behavior; Don't Shame It

"Shy people undervalue what they are—and overvalue what they're not."

– Author Dorothy Sarnoff

I was in a local restaurant, sitting at table full of fellow professionals, awaiting our orders, chatting about our recent successes and comparing notes on various projects. We'd purposely chosen an off-hour so the dining room wasn't very full and we had the pleasure of having our particular section all to ourselves. As happens with any group of big personalities, our conversation got loud and it wasn't long before we were all laughing, joking and maintaining multiple conversations across the table.

At first, I barely noticed the 20-something couple that was being seated in our section. That changed in a moment as the young man caught his shoe on the edge of the carpet. Arms wind milling, he went sprawling to the ground, but not before knocking over a tray of dirty dishes that also went clattering to the ground.

Everyone looked at him in stunned silence for a moment, and then a friend at our table jumped up to help him. The mortified young man lurched up off the ground, ignoring my friend's outstretched hand and plopped down at the table next to us.

"Sir, are you alright?" The hostess' expression of concern only seemed to deepen his embarrassment, evidenced by his mumbled, "Fine, thanks."

Our conversation started up again but I could hear the young man lambasting himself, "I'm such an idiot. I can't believe I did that. Everyone's looking at me."

I understood why he was upset, but was saddened to hear how hard he was being on himself. He didn't let up. "Moron. What a klutz."

That's when his girlfriend spoke up. She said, *"Don't talk about my boyfriend that way."*

What a perfect response! However, the young man kept at it. "It's embarrassing! I'm always doing stupid stuff like this...."

"I understand it's embarrassing; and calling yourself names won't help."

"I can call myself anything I want," the young man countered.

"You're right, you can. Let me ask you this, though. Would you just sit here and let someone else call you a moron or an idiot?"

"No. I wouldn't let anyone talk to me that way!"

"If you wouldn't let anyone else talk to you that way, why do you let yourself? Don't you deserve to treat yourself with the same respect you give others?"

The young man snorted in agreement. His girlfriend had a good point! What a powerful question she had asked.

- Don't we deserve the respect from ourselves that we expect from others?
- If we wouldn't allow a stranger to call us names, why do we call ourselves Stupid! Moron! Idiot?
- Does it help when we verbally abuse ourselves? Does it change things? Make them better? Or does it make us feel worse?

Flogging is Not a Yoga Pose

"I must learn to love the fool in me, the one who feels too much, talks too much, takes too many chances, wins sometimes and loses often, lacks self-control, loves and hates, hurts and gets hurt, promises and breaks promises, laughs and cries."
– Theodore Issac Rubin

I spent the rest of our lunch reflecting on what I'd learned from this couple. In yoga, there is no room in the studio for judgment, from others or ourselves. Bringing negative energy into that serene space is profoundly counterproductive. Yogis never criticize, only correct and encourage students to appreciate and improve upon what they are capable of that day.

Self-talk, if there is any at all is strictly positive and growth-oriented. You must be forgiving of yourself in yoga because there will always be something out of reach; a pose, a smooth transition, a regulation of breath, a depth of serenity.

Each element can always be improved upon and if you are truly pushing yourself, you will always have moments where you lose your rhythm for a moment, wobble during a transition, or struggle with a pose.

When you wobble, bumble, or stumble while selling, shape your behavior through positive self-talk rather than shaming it with recriminations. Use the following questions to help you plan how you will correct this common habit:

- What did you say to yourself the last time you made a mistake?
- Would you tolerate someone else speaking to you the way you spoke to yourself?
- What did you gain through your self-talk?
- How would you want someone else to encourage you or support you when you've made a mistake?
- What would you gain by speaking to yourself with the same regard and respect you might hear from your closest friend?

Action Plan for Chapter 17

"When you're sad; learn something."
– The Wizard, Merlin, in Camelot

The next time you make a mistake, remember: flogging is not a *Sales Yoga* pose. Beating yourself up with words, thoughts or actions serves no purpose other than to prolong the pain and the recovery time. Evaluate your self-talk as if your internal voice was a friend, family member or partner. What would you want to hear from them in your moment of vulnerability? As Merlin pointed out, instead of feeling sad, learn something.

Poses to Hold/ Poses to Fold

- *Fold: "I'm such an idiot. I can't believe I tripped in front of everyone."*
- **Hold: "That was really embarrassing and I bet everyone in this room has done exactly what I just did at some point or another."**
- *Fold: "Nice job dummy, you even got paid to screw that up."*
- **Hold: "I wish I could have done that differently and next time I'll know what to avoid."**
- *Fold: "I can't believe I just blew that. What the heck am I doing here? I'm such a fraud."*
- **Hold: "I can do better than this. I know I am capable of more and I'm going to do better next time."**

Chapter 18:
Be Clear that Money is a Priority, Not a Resource

"The safest way to double your money is to fold it over and put it in your pocket."

– Kin Hubbard

We all want money, which is why I wonder why no one seems to have any when a salesperson comes along. Why is it that people appear to have cash, but profess an empty pocket when asked?

It's because money is a priority, not a resource.

Let me explain....

I was sitting with a 20-something business professional named Melinda, who was talking with me about how tight money was for her. She was clearly frustrated with her current employment, stating that she wasn't being paid enough; they didn't value her and was feeling the pinch in her daily life.

While I could intellectually connect with what Melinda was saying, I couldn't help but notice the $5 Frappuccino in her hand during our conversation. I began to wonder how she defined money; as a resource or a priority? So, I started asking questions.

"Melinda, what would you do if you had extra money?"

"Well, a lot of things. But if I had the choice, I'd go on a vacation. I haven't been on one in a long time."

"Okay. How much do you think it would cost?"

"Well," Melinda said, "I would go with my boyfriend and I don't expect him to pay for it all. I would pay my part. I guess we could have a nice vacation for around $1,500. I already know where I'd want to go."

I could see that she was getting excited about just the idea of a vacation so I guessed that the time with her boyfriend, away from work was pretty important to her.

"Great! So, if I found your $1500, you'd be able to go on this vacation?"

"Yeah! That would be amazing. What do you have in mind?"

"I know just where we can find this $1500. Let's do some quick math, okay? How many days a week do you get a Frappuccino?"

"Um, typically six if not seven days a week...why?"

"Okay, let's call it six. So, about 300 days per year, you get a Frappuccino. And how much does it cost you?"

"Well, about $5 and change. I always get the Venti."

"Congratulations. There's your $1500!"

Melinda looked confused so I explained.

"Money is not a resource, it's a priority. So far, you've made buying a Frappuccino every day a priority, enough of a priority to find the money for it and that's perfectly fine. Now, you want to go on a vacation. And if I read you right, you want the vacation more than you want daily Frappuccino's. Am I right?"

"Well, yeah. A vacation would be wonderful and it certainly wouldn't hurt to cut back on the coffee."

"Okay, good. If your drinks are $5 a piece and you stopped drinking them tomorrow and saved the money instead, by this time next year, you'd be on vacation."

"Wow, I'd never thought about it that way."

Now, in the story of Melinda, we're talking about someone who is early in their career, making between $30,000 - $40,000 per year. She has a limited amount of disposable income and will probably put a great deal of effort into prioritizing that money. Especially, once she starts conceptualizing money as a priority and not a resource.

Imagine the reprioritization that could happen with a company pulling in 100, 1000 or 10,000 times that amount of capital. When you are selling to a company and they tell you they don't have enough money, you have to shake that off. What they're really telling you is that *spending money on you is not a priority*.

Your job as a salesperson is to help people sell themselves on why your product or service is a top priority. Please notice that I say, "Sell themselves." They will always believe themselves, and only sometimes believe you.

Remember that the practice of *Sales Yoga* is always focused on the buyer and their needs. Your task is to be mindful of what the customer sees as their priorities and help them shift these to their benefit.

The holiday shopping season in 2012 is another excellent example of this concept. Because stores decided to open up with holiday deals on Thanksgiving Day rather than midnight on Black Friday, many people missed Thanksgiving dinner because they were waiting in line at those stores.

The New York Times quoted a woman who was furious with her husband for missing Thanksgiving dinner because he had been in line at an electronics store trying to save $40 on a new TV. He had prioritized this deal above his family get-together and she was not impressed. While she seemed shocked, I was not. People are constantly driven by their priorities.

We all have much to do, much we'd like to buy and most of us do not have unlimited time and money. The result of that is prioritization based on our own individual value system. While one person's choice may seem odd to some of us, like missing dinner to go buy a TV, others may see that as a perfectly reasonable decision based on the importance they place on both the TV and what they want to do with that saved $40.

The next time you are with a prospect or a client...look around.

- What kinds of things do they spend money on?
- Are there solar panels on the covered parking bays?
- Are there gourmet coffee machines in the break rooms or vending machines in the hallways?
- Are all their documents electronic, do they keep paper backups or is it a hardcopy business environment?
- Are the plants real, silk or no plants at all?

There will be small and large clues all around you to let you know how money is prioritized in that particular business so you can make the appropriate and necessary adjustments.

Action Plan for Chapter 18

"You don't close a sale; you open a relationship."
– Professional speaker Patricia Fripp

We've discussed before that *Sales Yoga* is a way of life, not just a way you do business. There will be moments when you'll find yourself ready to make some changes. Your personal exploration, while practicing *Sales Yoga*, will likely lead you toward practicing a life with more integrity, continuity, clarity and balance.

In your own life, think of two or three situations where you really wanted to do something, or buy something. This could be a trip you wanted to take, a car you wanted to buy, or a piece of technology that you really desired.

How did that level of prioritization impact your ability to come up with the money?

When considering a reprioritization of money, time is going to play a big factor in whether or not your adjustments feel like a sacrifice. The longer you go without something, in order to gain another, the higher the probability that this will feel like a sacrifice. One way to lessen that experience is to find a less expensive temporary or permanent replacement and work with the difference.

I love this quote from Amazon's Jeff Bezos. "At the end of the day, looking back at our life, you want to have minimized the number of regrets you have. That's what should drive us—not how much money we have. It's regrets that will haunt us in the end." He's right. When I think of things that are a priority in my life, I only think about how grateful I am for them, I never think of how much they cost. How about you?

You may be surprised that I'm asking you to focus on your relationship with money. Unless you shift from viewing money as a priority instead of resource, you'll have a difficult time helping a client to do the same.

Now, when considering this approach with your own prospects, ask yourself these questions:

---

1. How can I help my prospects see my service or product as a priority over other potential investments?
2. What do they spend money on that might be better spent on my product or service?
3. How do I help them see money as a priority rather than a resource?
4. What *Launching Questions* can I ask to get them to sell themselves on shifting their priorities?

Chapter 19:
Sell the Front of the Box, Not the Features

"If I look confused it's because I'm thinking."

– Samuel Goldwyn

If your customers look confused, it could be because you're trying to sell features before they're ready for them.

Last year, I was in the tea aisle of Whole Foods grocery store. If you've never been to the tea aisle of Whole Foods, it's a plethora of color, size and shape. They have more tea than I ever knew existed; it's truly a thing of beauty...and a potential sales nightmare for individual suppliers.

Manufacturers have learned to compete in this cornucopia by packaging their tea in boxes, tins and containers of all colors, sizes and shapes to attract your attention.

There was a woman standing in the aisle gazing at the wall of tea, clearly focused on the task at hand. I could empathize with her dilemma. As I watched her consider her options, I noticed that she was scanning the shelves, occasionally picking up a box or tin, checking out the back and then either placing the item in her cart or putting it back on the shelf.

I watched a bit longer, curious about the system she had going. Eventually my curiosity won out and I approached her, trying to construct an opening statement that wouldn't make me look like a stalker.

"Excuse me, I hope I'm not intruding but I was noticing how you were looking at tea. I'm a consultant. My clients are always interested in finding out what packaging helps a product pop off a shelf. I noticed what you were doing…can I ask you about it?"

Apparently she didn't mind sharing her tea selection process because she enthusiastically agreed.

"I noticed you're very particular with what you're looking for. Why?"

"Well," she started, "They're out of my normal brand, so I have to find a replacement."

As I looked back at the wall-o-tea, I couldn't imagine there was a single item on the planet missing from these shelves but I took her word for it.

"I've decided I might as well experiment with some new flavors and brands. Maybe there's something better than what I was buying before."

"Okay, and how are you going to pick?"

"Well, I like a very robust tea so I'm looking for cues—pictures or words—on the front of the box that tell me it might be full-flavored."

"Okay, I noticed that when you found one before, you would always check the back."

"Right. I know the ingredients in my old tea and they list them on the back. That's how it works. The front of the box grabs my interest and the back of the box helps me finalize my decision. Simple as that."

Tea Lady helped confirm for me that people want an experience first; that packaging comes before features. The same phenomenon occurs on a larger scale, as well. Imagine if you were working in the staffing and recruiting industry.

People can't be put in boxes, but if they could, what would you put on the outside of the box?

- *Skills?*
- *Education?*
- *Experience?*

Nope!

It's always accomplishments. Think about this from the perspective of the person hiring. They might look at the skills and experience but what they're really looking for is what those skills and experience can do for their company. Nothing tells you that better than previous accolades.

If you have three, equally qualified individuals standing side-by-side, what will catch your attention and pull your interest is previous recognition of excellence. It's your quality guarantee. Just because one product, a person in this example, has a certain set of ingredients (skills) doesn't mean they necessarily combine well for a good experience.

Resumes, websites, product packaging, brochures, even interviews should all be focused with the model of accomplishments first. Share with the prospect how your particular brand of acclaimed excellence has helped others. Buyers relate best to how people in their situation have benefited from your product or service.

In *Sales Yoga*, we live with the mantra of: "Say little, ask a lot." We ask lots of questions to understand the customer's needs, to diagnose their pains and to understand the value they want to receive. Then and only then, after we develop a clear understanding of our customer, do we "say the little" part. We sell just like the tea box: a picture and a few words on the front with the ingredients and nutritional information on the back.

Action Plan for Chapter 19

"A conversation is a dialogue; not a monologue."
– Truman Capote

Here's how that conversation might sound if you turn it into a dialogue by asking the right questions.

Scott: "Thank you for taking the time to meet with me. I've done my homework on your company but I'd like to hear from you about your company's needs? What are you looking for?"

Buyer: "Well, right now we're looking to do a software overhaul. The old system isn't holding up and we need to make some changes before the old system starts causing more problems than we can fix."

Scott: "Okay, tell me more about why you originally chose that system?"

Buyer: "Sure, we chose that one when we were smaller; it could handle the traffic, had the features we needed and allowed us to be flexible in the way we delivered various pieces of information to our clients. Actually, I wish we could stay with this one but it's just not practical."

Scott: "Really, why do you say that?"

Buyer: "Well, we have a number of employees and it's going to be a logistical nightmare to retrain everyone on a new program. Everyone is familiar with this program; its user-friendly, the company had great customer service whenever we had a question but what I really loved was that you could personalize the settings to make the program your own. That was really nice."

Scott: "I can see how that would be a point of interest. Before we discuss some options, what else should I know about your software needs?"

Buyer: "Well, it would be really great if someone were willing to come out and do group training to kick-start the transition."

Scott: "Great! I have several options, one of which performed very well with another client of mine that is similar to your firm. This software program was just rated #1 in its class, especially since it is scalable for organizations your size, yet still offers the ability for personalized setting. The company recently received a J.D. Power award for their outstanding customer support. In addition, during my last three installations, each customer raved at the effectiveness of the training program."

Buyer: "That sounds like just what I'm looking for."

Scott: "Good. Let me show you some of the details (features)."

The next time you are in a sales conversation, sell the front of the box first and see how your buyer responds.

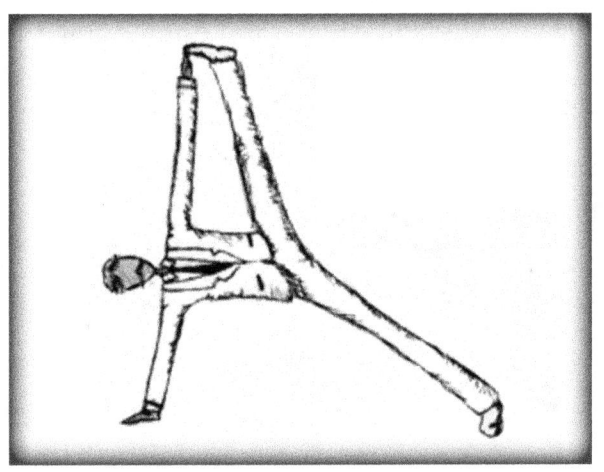

Chapter 20:
Provocative *Launching Questions* Pay Off

"To seduce almost anyone, ask for and listen to his opinions."

– Malcolm Forbes

Sue, an experienced sales pro, had been contacting Jerry for several months, yet Jerry wouldn't give her the time of day.

It was driving her *crazy*. She knew Jerry was doing business with her competitor. She also knew her company could provide better options; but without an open line of communication, she would never have a chance to earn Jerry's trust or his account.

Week after week, Sue would call. Most of the time, she left a voice message that was never returned. A couple times, Jerry actually answered the phone. She quickly introduced herself and asked for a short meeting. Both times, Jerry said, "No thanks."

It was tempting to point out in her voice messages *all* the things her company did better than the competition. She knew, though, that a one-way sales pitch (or a sales dump as a colleague calls it) would make Jerry less likely to respond, so she resisted that urge and stayed focused on gaining an in-person meeting. Sue knew, especially in this instance, that a face-to-face meeting was the best way to form a mutually rewarding working relationship.

Much to her (pleasant) surprise, Jerry finally said, "Yes."

"Sue, I am impressed with your persistence. I respect that you're trying to win me over. I'm pretty happy with whom we work with now, but I'll tell you what…if you come in, I'll give you 10 minutes."

Sue set up the meeting. She was ecstatic to finally have the face-to-face appointment she'd been waiting for, and working for.

As soon as she hung up the phone with Jerry, she called me. "Scott, you've been teaching me to use *Attractive Persistence* and it has finally paid off. Thank you! If you hadn't been advising me to keep at it, I would have given up a long time ago and this never would have happened."

I told her, "See what I mean? Jerry wasn't annoyed by your persistence; he was impressed. As long as you're consistent and respectful when you follow up with potential clients, they often end up appreciating it."

Sue said, "The question now is: How do I convince Jerry to work with us instead of our competitor? He's made it clear he likes them. What do I do?"

"Well, the way I see it, he's working with *them now* because he doesn't know his company needs *you yet*. The good news is, you know your products and services are better. Let's focus on helping him to *convince himself* to work with you instead of them."

"But I've only got 10 minutes. How can I possibly close this deal in 10 minutes?"

"Sue, you don't have 10 minutes and you're not going to try to 'close this deal.' Researchers believe we only have *nine seconds* to capture people's attention. That means you've got to engage Jerry with the first thing you say, before his attention wanders and you become 'just another salesperson.'

"This is one of the reasons *Sales Yoga* works so well. *Sales Yoga* is always about what engages the buyer. What does your buyer need? What do they want? What problems does his company have that you can solve?

"Ask yourself, 'What matters to Jerry?' You're not going to *pitch*. You're going to ask short, nine-second or less, provocative *Launching Questions* to engage him from the get-go. What will make them provocative is not just their brevity, but their ability to get him to think more deeply."

Sue and I strategized a variety of provocative *Launching Questions* she could ask that would be relevant for Jerry. I also emphasized that she was given 10 minutes, and 10 minutes only, and that it was crucial for her to work within that time limit.

I told Sue, "Running long is one of the quickest ways to offend people and lose trust because it's a form of arrogance. It tells people you can't be counted on to keep commitments; that you primarily care about what *you* want, not what *they* want."

Sue agreed to interrupt herself, mid-sentence if necessary, to honor her time agreement. We then rehearsed a "mock meeting" so Sue would be comfortable walking into Jerry's office. We didn't want her to be robotic or nervous. We wanted her to be well prepared so she could relax, think on her feet and exude a warm confidence.

The next week Sue arrived early at Jerry's gleaming glass tower office building so she'd have time to compose herself instead of feeling rushed. She looked around appreciatively at the impressive lobby, gleaming mahogany doors and luxurious furniture. Instead of feeling intimidated, she sat in a comfortable chair in a private corner of the lobby and did some discrete deep yogic breathing exercises we had practiced together.

Within a few minutes, she felt calm, centered and raring to go. She walked into her meeting a minute early, confidently shook Jerry's hand, exchanged "Nice to meet you's," and jumped in to her first provocative *Launching Question*, "Jerry, under what circumstances would you consider a different provider?"

Jerry thought for a minute and then offered his answer. Sue listened carefully and *integrated* his response into her next question to give him an opportunity to expand upon what he'd just said. Each time he spoke, she responded with a question that mined his comments and helped him explain what he meant more clearly and deeply.

Right before her allotted time was up, Sue kept her promise. She interrupted herself and said, "Jerry, you made it clear I had 10 minutes of your time...."

Jerry came back with, "Sue, don't worry about that. I want to keep going." He enthusiastically described his company's challenges for another half hour, and didn't stop until his secretary knocked on his door to remind him of his next appointment.

He looked at Sue a bit sheepishly and confessed, "To tell you the truth, Sue, when I gave you 10 minutes, it was more of a courtesy than anything else. I really didn't think we needed to make a change, but you've proven you're different. You've shown more of an understanding of our needs in this short meeting than some of my current providers have in years. You know what? I'm going to give you a shot."

Sue left that meeting thrilled, and called me to celebrate her good news. "This is incredible. Those provocative *Launching Questions* worked!"

"Sue, of course they worked! First, you centered yourself with that yogic breathing so you were focused instead of frazzled. Then, you made the conversation about him and his needs instead of it being about you 'trying to close a deal.'"

What Sue learned was this: When Jerry had given her a brief 10 minutes to talk, he was really indicating he only had that much time and tolerance to listen to her. He thought *she'd* be doing the talking and *he'd* be doing the listening.

Instead, she did just the opposite.

When *Jerry* had a chance to do the talking and Sue was the one doing the listening, he suddenly had all the time in the world. By giving him a chance to go deep into his company's needs, he was able to expound on what they wanted in a way he never had before. Sue's willingness to *listen instead of lecture* won him over.

The point?

People don't want to be talked at. They want to be listened to.

People don't want to be "pitched," they want to be engaged. And, one of the best ways to engage people (especially ones who are already buying from a competitor) is by asking a provocative *Launching Question* such as, "Under what circumstances would you consider another provider?" or, "How could we make you happier?" and then listening carefully to what's being said and integrating that into follow-up questions. When you do this, you give prospects a chance to identify needs that aren't being met and problems that aren't being solved.

Another bonus is that, instead of being satisfied with the status quo, provocative *Launching Questions* help prospective clients explore and articulate better options they haven't even considered.

Furthermore, a series of provocative *Launching Questions* combined with attentive listening keeps the focus on your prospects, which keeps them engaged from start to finish.

Think about it. How long has it been since someone has given you an opportunity to go deep into how you feel about an issue? How long has it been since someone focused solely on what you wanted, what you needed, what you thought? How long has it been since someone asked thought-provoking questions that caused you to re-examine your thinking and arrive at new conclusions that improved your circumstances?

It is extremely rare, which makes it extremely welcome.

That is why short, provocative questions, combined with deep listening and integrative follow-up, is one of the best things you can do to make people feel important and understood, and it's one of the best things you can do to turn coercion into collaboration.

Remember, the longer you talk, the more people tune out. Replace pitches (one-way communication) with provocative *Launching Questions* (two-way communication) if you want to genuinely engage people and capture their interest.

And remember what we learned from Sue and Jerry's story. Consistent, respectful, attractive persistence pays off. Taking a few moments to do deep yogic breathing before an important meeting pays off. Asking provocative *Launching Questions* and listening carefully pays off. Giving prospects your full focus pays off. And giving people an opportunity to go deep and identify unmet needs your company can address better than their current provider pays off too...for you *and* for your new client.

Action Plan for Chapter 20

*"Successful people ask better questions,
and as a result, they get better answers."*
– Anthony Robbins

During your next sales call or meeting, transform your approach from a one-way pitch to a two-way conversation by using provocative *Launching Questions*.

Remember to listen intently to the needs that are being articulated so you can integrate that into your next question and help people uncover what their organization wants but doesn't currently have.

Your first provocative *Launching Question* can be similar to the one Sue used with Jerry, "Under what circumstances would you consider another provider?"

Sample topics for additional *Launching Questions* include:

- **General inquiry**
  How can I help right now?
- **Budget cuts/adjustments**
  How are recent budget cuts affecting your department?
- **Industry trends and disruptions**
  Which industry trends are impacting you the most?
- **Outsourcing vs. insourcing**
  What would happen if you implemented insourcing?
- **Collapsed/condensed time frames**
  How would a condensed production schedule improve product turnaround?
- **Price vs. value**
  Under what circumstances would value have more impact than price?
- **Personnel needs**
  Where are your personnel needs the greatest? How is that impacting productivity?
- **Changes in operational procedures or policies**
  In what ways have policy changes transformed your business model?

Chapter 21:
Persist ... Gently

"I am extraordinarily patient, provided I get my own way in the end."

– Former Prime Minister of England, Margaret Thatcher

An integral part of being a Sales Yogi is diplomatically building your brand and staying *top of mind*. You need to do both to sustain your business.

I was in Texas a few summers ago, running a workshop with a global engineering company. I'd been called in to work with their employees on a number of my *Sales Yoga* poses including: *Attractive Persistence*. This plan is designed to support consistent brand presence to keep the company and its services top of mind.

Now, one of the more frustrating experiences a speaker can have is when someone in the workshop is committed to being contradictory. Brad was one such individual. Rather than ask questions or make statements for the purpose of learning and clarification, he simply wanted to show everyone else in the room how smart he thought he was.

When I said left, he said right. When I introduced a technique he would immediately announce why it would *never* work. I'd even been warned about Brad by the CEO before arriving on site. As expected, when I rolled out *the Attractive Persistence Plan*, Brad just rolled his eyes.

"Okay Brad, let's have some fun with this. I'll make you a bet. Let's pick a prospect that you know is using services like yours, but just isn't using you."

"Okay," Brad said. "I'll take that bet."

"Great. You're going to follow this *Attractive Persistence Plan* for a period of time, and I'll bet you $20 that they will eventually call back. If you follow this plan of strategic phone calls, visits when appropriate, emails and collateral material to help you stay top of mind, and be persistent, you will gain their business."

"Okay, Scott. You've got a deal. I'm looking forward to winning that $20 when this flops."

After the first few weeks, I asked Brad to send me an update. His emails only ever had two words: HA-HA. That obviously meant the prospect hadn't called back. Month two was the same thing. Brad checked in once or twice per month motivated by the opportunity to "prove me wrong." Months three and four were the same: HA-HA.

Month five was: "You wanna pay me now, Scott?"

"Just give it a little more time Brad. Be patient. You're building your brand."

Month six was nearly over with no emails. Just before the end of the month, I got a call from Brad. He was in a panic.

"You're not going to believe what happened!"

Of course, I knew exactly what happened. John, the manager of a major oil and gas company had called him back. Brad relayed the phone call to me, breathless and more than a little stunned:

"Number One, he said, 'Brad, I'm sorry I haven't called you back. I haven't needed to make a change but our circumstances are different now and I'd like you to come in and have a meeting with the boss.'"

Well, now I understood why Brad was out of breath.

"Scott, I've never even had a chance to talk to him. I didn't have to say anything. He had heard enough in my messages that he already decided that he wanted to meet with me. What should I do?"

Really?

"Brad, go to the damned meeting!"

Brad went to the meeting, sat down in front of the buyers (John and John's boss).

"Boss, let me tell you why Brad is here. He's clearly different. He's been calling me for the past six months now and in that time, he's left some pretty compelling messages about the benefits of their services and some of the things they've been able to do for their clients.

"I got the impression over time that this company is very invested in their clients. I looked at their website, did some research and they clearly stand out. It's not a question of *if* I want to work with him but rather *how* we are going to do that at this point. That's why I wanted you here."

They closed the deal in that first meeting.

Typically, it takes three or four or five meetings. This deal was closed in the first meeting because the buyer was there, the buyer's boss was there and Brad had built up his brand so well in John's mind that he really didn't need to sell anymore.

Staying top of mind is about being nimble and quick with our sales technique. In the electronic age, it is easy to see email as a quick way to distribute information, make contacts and relay messages. Unfortunately, what gets lost in the email is the nimble and more personal nature of verbal communication. Email is quick, but it's not nimble.

Once you put those words down on the page, you lock yourself into however the other person interprets those words and chooses to respond. There is little opportunity to create an interpersonal bond or connection and no chance of gaining their attention if they just trash your email.

Whether we like it or not, phone calls (and meetings, for that matter), while they can be uncomfortable at times, are the best way to be flexible and quick in your conversation. Using the techniques we've already discussed to be efficient and precise in your questions and statements can go a long way toward building your brand before you ever meet face-to-face.

When it finally came time for John to call Brad back, John needed very little additional information about the potential deal. Brad, through his carefully constructed, *Attractive Persistence Plan*, helped John develop an understanding of the company and their offered services without ever having a live conversation.

The premise of the *Attractive Persistence Plan* is about being consistent but not irritating. We focus on being brief, polite and interesting.

- **Brief:** Message no longer than 30 seconds total. This includes a brief introduction, a compelling question or statement (such as mentioning that you just saved a similar company over a million dollars) and your contact information (repeated twice to ensure accuracy).
- **Polite:** Do not bash the competition, chastise the prospect for not calling you back, or have an arrogant attitude or tone. Do call persistently, which for many people means about once each week.
- **Interesting:** Make a different statement or ask a different question in each of your messages. Your questions and statements should be *provocative*; the kind of question or statement that would stick in someone's mind. Your goal is to begin to deliver value from the very start, and that begins with leaving valuable, interesting messages.

When you persist at poses in yoga, you become stronger and more limber. When you persist in *Sales Yoga*, you are being a strong advocate for the customers you can help. The importance of persistence is in showing the prospect that they are important to you. Just like showing up to work on time; contacting prospects in a persistent and consistent way implies a commitment to the relationship, before it even starts.

Action Plan with Chapter 21

"We can do anything we want if we stick to it long enough." – Helen Keller

Let's follow the example with Brad.

---

1. Pick a prospect that you know is buying, but not buying from you.
2. Commit to at least six months of an *Attractive Persistence Plan*.
3. Develop your Brief, Polite, and Interesting conversational material with an emphasis on strategic phone calls.
4. Prepare for both talking to a live person and leaving a message. While emails should not take the place of calls, these can be sent to supplement each call.
5. Generate enough material to be able to have a unique conversation or leave a different message. You can recycle after a while, but try not to revisit material in the same month.
6. Chose how often you are going to contact your prospect, keeping in mind that once a week is common.
7. Choose your reward!

Begin!

In case you were wondering, here's a sample message using the Brief, Polite, and Interesting format:

"Hello Peter, this is Scott with ABC Company. My number is 727-555-2211. Steven Jones recommended I contact you about the success we've had over the past three months for another company in your business. This included reducing time-to-fill by more than 50% in just six weeks' time. Again, my number is 727-555-2211. I'll be available for a return call until 5:00 pm today.

Chapter 22:
Do This When a Client Says, "I'm Sorry, There's Someone Else"

*"I can't give you the formula for success;
I can for failure; try to please everyone."*

– Bill Cosby

I got a call from an existing customer and they were contacting me for that reason all salespeople hate to get a phone call. They were calling to say there was somebody else. Another company had approached them, was offering the same deal for 5% less.

My client explained that they had to watch their budget and decided to seriously consider making a change. The customer further explained to me that he didn't really want to make a change, but if I couldn't meet that price, they would have to go with the other company.

Now of course, emotionally I'm feeling a bit betrayed, like I've just discovered that my partner has been having an affair, or that I'm being left at the altar! Rather than give in to the panic and betrayal, which are valid but unhelpful emotions, I grounded myself in my *Sales Yoga* practice.

"Yasir, I want to thank you for calling and being so candid with me. I'm curious. What would it make it worth staying with us, paying what you are now?"

There was a pregnant pause. He didn't just dismiss the question out of hand, which was a good sign.

"That's an interesting question…there is something…."

"Okay, would you like to talk about that now or later, at your office?"

I emphasized the casual, no-pressure, nature of this conversation. I didn't want Yasir to feel like I was desperate and going to chase him down. I had a dual goal with this approach:

1) Keep my anxiety to myself so the client doesn't get tense and want to end the conversation before it's truly done, and

2) Avoid making the client feel guilt for doing what any good businessperson would do in exploring their options and looking for the best deal for what *appears* to be equal value.

"Well you know Scott, our payables department has really been on us about getting longer payment terms to help us with our cash flow. If we had a bit longer, that might make it worth that 5%."

Using the integrative question technique, I simply said:

"Okay, what's longer?"

"Oh, I don't know. Maybe 10 more days?"

Yasir's voice had gone from conciliatory and resigned to hopeful in a matter of seconds. Now, instead of prompting me to adjust or lose him as a client, he's asking me for accommodations in order to maintain our relationship. This puts the power back in my hands and allows for a conversation in place of a "sales break up" phone call.

Yasir's company had always paid on time and often, in less than 30 days so his request was by no means unreasonable. I knew my supervisor would be glad to keep the account, especially for such a small adjustment. Now, I needed only one more integrative question to close the deal.

"If I can get you those 10 more days, then can we continue working together in the way we always have?"

"Yes, Scott. Thank you! That's such a relief. I really wasn't looking forward to the transition."

I remember ending that phone call with a smile on my face. Not only did we keep the client, we actually negotiated an agreement that cost us nothing and ended with the client paying us more than our competitors because of our flexibility. What I realized here was the value of allowing the client to sell *themselves* on an idea, rather than trying to do the heavy lifting, myself.

Remember: Buyers always believe themselves, but only sometimes believe you.

This is a key *Sales Yoga* concept and will guide your interactions and questions. Could you imagine how that conversation with Yasir might have gone had I panicked and tried to offer him things to get him to stay? I could have offered to meet my competitor's price, essentially underselling the value my company offered. I could have guessed at things he might have wanted and never would have come up with something as simple and painless as 10 more days on their payment terms.

Rather than jumping the gun and flinging ideas and concessions at my client, who already felt guilty for having to make the phone call, I helped him feel comfortable, understood and free to ask to get his needs met. Most salespeople would have stuttered, sputtered and spewed out a frantic plea:

"But Yasir, what about the past ten years of business together? What about the trust and value you've had with us. You don't know if those guys can give you what we can. That 5% could be a cut in quality not price! What if we added in some of our new services at a discounted rate? And yes, I can even talk to my supervisor about trying to match that decrease? Think about it."

Now, the client is uncomfortable, we're begging and both of us just want it to stop. While it seems like the right thing to do to try and win them back, we end up making the client feel embarrassed and culpable for our distress.

Remember, this isn't about you, it's about the client. By meeting your client's needs, you meet your own needs. Focusing on yourself rather than the client will only hurt your relationship in the long run and make them feel justified in going with someone else when the opportunity arises.

- What is your approach when a client calls with a counter offer?
- Are you prepared to have a conversation? Have you ever been caught off guard?
- How do you avoid compromising your value by lowering your price?
- What are some questions you might ask to open up the conversation?

Most people don't like change and really resist rocking the boat. When a client calls you to make a change, unless your service has been sub-par, it's pretty much a guarantee that they'd really rather not. This means that they'll jump at the chance to keep their business with you, as long as you approach them in a calm, reassuring and supportive way.

Salespeople are renowned for their "agenda," which puts people on guard long before they pick up the phone. Your job, as a *Sales Yoga* practitioner is to sooth their anxiety, balance the field and help your client get what they really want: the best of both worlds.

By asking integrative questions rather than making pressure-based statements, you can find out what it would take to keep your client. And, you strengthen your relationship by showing them that you care about their needs and are willing to make reasonable adjustments when needed.

Action Plan for Chapter 22

"I wish my mouth had a backup key." – popular Tweet

Has something gone wrong? In the heat of the moment, did you say or do something you wish you could take back? Do you wish your mouth had a backup key? Has a client said, "Sorry, there's someone else" or "I want out?"

If so, it's smart to develop a plan to use with clients when they call for a "sales break up." Have a basic plan for each of the possible reasons a client might make this phone call. Below is an example of a basic three-pronged action plan to help you develop your own, based on your business's resources and flexibility.

Sales Yoga Break Up Counter-Plan

1. Price
- "What would it make it worth staying with us, paying what you are now?"
- "If I can get you that, then can we continue working together?"

2. Value

    a. Quality

    b. Quantity

A) Quality Issue:
  - "What would our service/product look like if it met your quality standard?"
  - "If we can make those adjustments, then can we continue our relationship?"

B) Quantity Issue:

  - What are some services/products that could really impact your business and improve your experience?
  - We have some options:
    1) We can keep the price we have now for the services you're currently getting.
    2) We can incorporate the ____service you mentioned for 5% more, or
    3) We can incorporate the ____service and _____product for only 10% more. Which would you prefer?

3. Customer Service

  - What has it been like interacting with us?
  - What would it look like if you were completely at ease and comfortable with our representatives?
  - If our representatives could make those adjustments, could we continue our business together?
  - How about we meet at 2pm next Thursday to ensure that your experience has been improved?

Chapter 23:
Fire Clients Who Are Not a Match

*"We've got to follow through on our ideals,
or we betray something at the heart of who we are."*

– musician and activist Bono

There are moments in our lives when we have a choice—
honor our fears or honor our values. If we give into our fears
("How am I going to pay bills??") and go along with situations
that are not in alignment with our values, we, as Bono points out,
betray something at the heart of who we are.

Every salesperson, sometime, somewhere, will end up in a
no-win situation with a client. It could be that the client is not
acting with integrity. It could be that they're too demanding and
nothing you do ever satisfies them. It could be that they're not
paying their bills on time...or at all.

At that point, you have a choice. You can continue to tolerate
inappropriate behavior or you can draw the line and hold yourself and the people you deal with accountable for acting with
integrity.

That's the situation Todd was in. Todd was the CEO of a large national health care company that worked directly with various health care facilities. He was a hands-on leader and committed to his company after spending much of his career building this business from the ground, up.

At the time Todd hired me on retainer as his advisor in 2001, one of their largest accounts made up more than 60% of their business. Seeing this for the risk it was, one of the first things we began working on was diversifying market share to take the burden of success off of that single facility.

After some time, we managed to expand the company and that account until that single facility was less than 20%. They were still a substantial chunk but Todd was not as beholden to them as he once was.

While speaking with Todd about our progress he mentioned that this facility held an annual account review meeting, which was coming up soon. Each year, Todd and his Senior National Sales Manager would appear before a panel of stern-faced executives for what amounted to a public dressing-down for perceived shortcomings and excessive cost.

The panel would focus on everything they thought was "wrong" with the service Todd's company was providing. At the end of the review, Todd would walk out with his hat in his hand, head down, having just agreed to some kind of concession, like lowering his price to keep this client "happy" though there was clearly no satisfying them.

After Todd finished catching me up on the history of the "dreaded panel review" he started to smile.

"Todd," I said. "You're smiling. What are you thinking?"

"Scott," he replied, brightening by the second. "I don't have to take this 'summons to the principal's office' stuff. They're important, but we won't go under if we lose them, not anymore. I don't have to take this beating and I'm excited. I've never been excited about this review but this time, I finally feel like I have some power."

I was intrigued.

"Tell me Todd, what do you have in mind?"

"Well, I've wanted to fire these guys for years but the impact would have been irreparable. That's not true anymore. We would survive it; it would be tough to give up that revenue, but we'd be okay. I think I want to fire these guys. But, can I do that? We've had this account for years; they're almost 20% of our business. This sounds crazy...and more than a little scary."

"Todd," I said, leaning in to make sure I had his attention. "Fire them! They don't deserve you. You don't deserve to be treated like this and you've done the hard work to ensure that you don't have to suffer in silence any more. We can talk about your delivery later but do this for me right now: close your eyes, take a deep breath and imagine firing this client and never having to take this abuse from them again."

Todd followed my instructions and, just as I'd expected, a serene smile came across his face and he started to laugh.

"How do you feel?"

"I feel free...powerful...fearless."

For the next few weeks, Todd and I did our homework, practiced the delivery and prepared for the "dreaded account review." When the day finally came, Todd walked into that review calm, collected, present and ready to let go. He introduced himself, thanked the panel for being there, and jumped right in before the panel had the chance to start in on him.

"Before we go any further, I'd like to discuss our history together. I've noticed the last few years that you've been unhappy with the services my company provides and we have been unable to remedy the issues.

"We're letting you down, to be blunt. So today, I've come here prepared to help you transition to another provider, one that can meet your needs and alleviate your dissatisfaction. I'm here to get out of your way and I suggest we make today's meeting about that transition."

Todd, as he relayed the events to me later, said:

"Scott, you should have seen the looks on their faces. They were shocked! Like jaws on the ground, stopped in their tracks, *shocked*. It was incredible. And the best part was, they actually spent the rest of the meeting trying to convince *me* to stay on board, and they agreed to pay *more* while making concessions that will make our working relationship better than it's ever been!"

Todd went into that review, listened intently and said very little. They had dialogue with no convincing, inducing or influencing. He took a stand, prepared to let them go and in doing so, took his power back. This is the essence of *Sales Yoga*; it isn't about being slick, having canned lines, or being super energetic and in their face.

Sales Yoga is about conversations conducted with presence, poise and purpose. You don't have to dominate the room to be the one in control. People who are truly prepared to cope with the consequences of their actions are always the ones with the power.

Rather than acting out of anger or fear, we can recognize that we have a choice. Oftentimes we can feel powerless in a given situation, but that is rarely actually true. There is always a choice, in any situation, and, while we may not have control over the actions of others, we always have control over our own actions and *re*actions. Detecting choice is about expanding our mind beyond our assumptions and perceived limits.

Here's an extreme example: In a mugging, we may think "I had no choice; the guy had a gun so I handed over my wallet." However, we do have two options: hand over the wallet or risk getting shot. The second option was simply unacceptable and, therefore dismissed without conscious thought. For Todd, his sense of powerlessness was connected to the belief that he had no choice but to endure the facility's abuse.

We now know that he *did* have control of the situation. It was simply a time-sensitive and circumstantial control. And, instead of indefinitely surrendering control, Todd gathered his resources, expanded his business and changed the game as soon as he had the means to do so.

- When you look at the customers you work with, how does it make you feel to stand with them every day?
- Which of them no longer feels "worth it," whether that is a result of their abusiveness, unreasonable demands, poor payment history, or low profitability?
- In a "perfect world" what would your client list be comprised of?
- What would it take to get you from what you have now, to what you really want?
- How would you prepare yourself, and your company, to let go of your *VIC's* (Very Insulting Clients) while still making that transition in the client's best interest?

By the way, I actually fired a yoga instructor one time.

I showed up for my regular class after a few weeks of travel, only to discover my favorite instructor had moved. I can only imagine this unexpected departure had left the studio in a bind and they hadn't had time to find a quality replacement because this new instructor was the exact opposite of our previous encouraging "coach" instructor.

This new instructor seemed more intent on impressing us than leading us.

He spent the first couple minutes of class listing his credentials and proudly reeling off the names of a couple famous studios he claimed to have taught at. Then, after only a few warm-up poses, he started right into some very demanding poses.

My fellow yoga students and I swapped concerned looks. We were taken aback by his brash, egotistical, insensitive manner that was the opposite of what we'd come to appreciate about our former instructor.

Over the next 15 minutes, things got worse, not better. He rushed through the poses. When one of the students spoke up and asked him to slow down, he rudely told her, "If you can't keep up, maybe you should stick to the basic class."

Whoa. I didn't know if he was having a bad day or what, but there was no excuse for him insulting a student.

Enough! I got up, collected my things, went to the front desk and asked to see the manager. I told her, "I'm not 'complaining,' however I wanted to bring to your attention that this new instructor is not up to the standard of excellence you're known for." I then reported what had happened and said, "I thought you'd appreciate an opportunity to take corrective action."

The manager thanked me, and the instructor was let go.

The point? It doesn't serve anyone to suffer in silence. If you can read the writing on the wall and see that a relationship is not a good fit; speak up and take action. It doesn't help anyone for you to settle for a verbally abusive or inefficient relationship. Review the steps in the Action Plan to decide how you can be proactive in terminating an unhealthy relationship.

Action Plan for Chapter 23

"The better we feel about ourselves; the fewer times we have to knock someone down to feel tall" – Collette

When we find ourselves in an uncomfortable or dissatisfying relationship, we can remember that the power is ours, we simply need to commit to the time and effort it takes to use that power.

Here are 10 step-by-step questions to ask yourself and your company when you are feeling powerless, stuck and mistreated:

---

1. What are my options, from the most extreme to the most realistic?
2. Of all my options for change, which one is the best combination of practicality and positive outcome?
3. Why haven't I made this change already?
4. What would it take to prepare for this change? Time? Money? Resources?
5. How can I support myself/company while we prepare for this transition?
6. What will it look like when we're ready to make a change?
7. How will I present this change to my client so the transition is in their best interest?
8. What changes will they have to make in order for me to consider continuing the relationship?
9. How long will I give them to make those changes before I continue with my plan to transition the relationship to someone else?
10. If the transition becomes necessary, what steps will I take to make it happen in a way that honors our needs and those of the client?

Chapter 24:
Always Be Collaborating

"PUT THAT COFFEE DOWN! Coffee is for closers."

– Blake, the movie Glengarry Glen Ross

I just saw a replay of a clip of a *Saturday Night Live* (SNL) skit with Alec Baldwin playing the Head Elf in a spinoff of the sales classic, *Glengarry Glen Ross*.

This iconic sales movie from the early 90's sported an all-star cast of Alec Baldwin, Al Pacino and Jack Lemmon, to name a few. In the original movie, they were the stereotypical salesmen with the stereotypical sales manager or Sales Boss.

The heavy-handed, threatening manager would barge in to the office demanding productivity:

"Step up or you're done!"

"Hit the quotas or you're fired!"

These threats and demands are still common today in the sales work environment. I walk in to sales organizations all the time and witness first hand, this heavy-handed, domination-focused approach.

I understand that organizations have to set standards in order for people to keep their seats or lose them, but there is a big difference between encouraging a goal and threatening a failure. It's all about the context, delivery and provided support.

In this SNL skit, Alec Baldwin played the Head Elf in charge of Santa's Workshop. He shouted and threatened and demanded that those little elves meet their toy quota or lose their jobs! He even shouted out an adapted version of the ABC (Always Be Closing) with "Always Be Cobbling!"

I couldn't help but laugh at the skit and relate. I've had a boss like that; many of us have, and it's horrible to work in that kind of negative environment. If the SNL scenario were real, could you imagine how those toys would turn out? The nasty attitude of the Head Elf would roll downhill to the elves, to be certain.

I would bet those toys would have sharp edges, broken parts and parts missing, all together! And, when the kids got those toys? I'm sure they'd scream and cry and blame Santa and their parents for their misfortune.

Domination rolls downhill.

When a sales manager or supervisor is dominating and aggressive with his or her employees, the employees have to transfer that negative energy elsewhere, they may take it out on each other, their friends, family and it may even creep in to the way they interact with their clients.

When a threatening energy is used to motivate a salesperson, they are much more likely to use that same threatening and dominating energy when trying to convince a prospect to buy. Such an approach has been modeled by their supervisors and the behavior is transmitted from one relationship to another.

And, as Sweet Brown said in her YouTube video gone viral, "Ain't nobody got time for that."

What buyer out there wants to be dominated in a conversation?

Who wants to be controlled through threats and ultimatums at work?

The old model, the old paradigm is so broken, and yet, when people get frustrated, tired or confused, Sales Boss is what they fall back on. At sales training workshops, when I hear these same heavy-handed techniques being recommended, I sometimes see people buying in or talking about how good it felt to take that approach.

But, then I ask participants to imagine themselves as the buyer and I say,

"If you were the buyer, is this how you'd like to be approached? Is this how you would want to be treated?"

No one ever says yes. In fact, many of them look a little embarrassed when they realized that they use these techniques on others all the time, but would take offense if someone tried it on them. And yet, speakers who encourage this are revered.

Why?

Why do we maintain this double standard?

If you don't like it, don't do it to your prospects and clients. And stop doing it to employees.

Sales Yoga isn't just for the salesperson. It is best practiced at a leadership level, as well. Domination rolls downhill and if we're going to have a collaborative process with our clients and prospects, we also need to have one between managers and employees.

So what do we do?

The techniques used with prospects are just as effective when used with sales personnel. Employees will respond the same way to their bosses that buyers respond to salespeople when they anticipate that old school, heavy-handed sales approach. They will deploy their shields to avoid conflict and discomfort. So as a sales leader, you can use:

- *Mind Over Mouth*: Employees show loyalty to their employers when they feel valued and heard. Resisting the temptation to talk even though you are in the position of power can go a long way toward building and sustaining long-term positive relationships with your personnel.

- *HalfTalk*: Cutting down how much you say to your employees by half can encourage them to say more to you. Your salespeople are much more likely to keep listening to you, when they feel that you make the same effort to listen to them.

- **Mantras:** Developing Mantras that support your company mission statement can seem cheesy but actually does support a more cohesive work environment. When people are clear on the purpose, usefulness and value of their day-to-day work, they are less likely to burn out or jump ship to the competition.

- **Homework:** When you hold department meetings, you can prompt people to think of things to contribute to the meeting by sending them home the day before. Make a habit of directly asking for people's input randomly rotating who you call on. The goal is not to catch someone off guard, rather; you want to assure each employee that their opinion is valued. A structured system also leaves room for more hesitant people to make themselves heard when they might otherwise be drowned out.

- *Launch, Lead, or Lock*: Focusing on open ended, story-evoking questions (*Launching Questions*) allows people to overcome any anxiety they might have around authority and say things they might otherwise forget or skip over. Integrating their answers into your next question can help your employees feel heard and understood, creating a stronger relationship that benefits both of you.

Any *Sales Yoga* technique can be modified and implemented in a leadership position. Your goal as a manager is the same as the goal of a salesperson. You want to create an employee-centered, collaborative, open-communication relationship that withstands the test of time, competition and inevitable peaks and valleys in sales.

Action Plan for Chapter 24

"When people anger you; they conquer you."
– Toni Morrison

One more time: Domination rolls downhill. It's okay to set standards. It's okay to tell your salespeople what you expect for them to accomplish. Being clear with your expectations and how you plan to measure them is a great motivator when done correctly. However, what most managers forget to do is follow up with a question that involves the employee.

"How would you like to accomplish these goals?"

"When do you expect to have met these goals?"

"When would you like to meet again to re-strategize, if needed?"

"What are some of the more difficult or trying aspects of these goals?"

"What kind of support would help you when faced with any obstacles?"

"How would you prefer to be approached if things aren't going the way we'd like?"

Keep notes of their responses to your questions!

Pay attention to how your employees prefer to be worked with. They are just as important to you as your individual clients. This is what makes the integration of the principles of yoga into the practice of sales so powerful. Great yoga teachers, and great sales leaders, always pay attention to the needs of those with whom they work.

If you make a habit of individualizing your approaches to prospects, it would make sense that the same standard be applied to your salespeople. After all, you probably have fewer employees than they have clients. You can practice *Sales Yoga* too.

Chapter 25:
Don't Try to Force a
Downward Dog

"It's rare to find a consistently insightful person who is also an angry person. They can't occupy the same space. If anger moves in, generosity and creativity move out."

– Seth Godin

So Mike came to me, angry, like beat red angry. He was a sales manager who'd attended one of my workshops and really related to the *Sales Yoga* approach. He'd gone back to his company in the Midwest and presented some of the concepts he'd learned to his salespeople. But, he couldn't get them to do it! He wasn't just angry with them, he was angry with me.

So, Mike and I sat down and talked over what had happened. He explained that, after attending the workshop, he'd decided that his people needed to change their approach. He called a staff meeting and said,

"Okay, I went to a workshop and learned about this new approach."

He explained the concept of *HalfTalk* and allowing the prospect to sell themselves. Then he said,

"So, we're going to start doing things this way. Any questions? Good. Go do it!"

Oh dear. Without realizing it, Mike had tried the equivalent of a yoga teacher telling a group of students to do a difficult posture, such as a handstand, without discussing why and how to go about it.

"Okay, Mike. There's our problem. It's not the system that isn't working. It was the presentation. You didn't even spend time trying the old-school way of being the convincer, influencer or inducer. You pretty much walked in there and were the dictator."

Mike didn't look terribly pleased with my observation. Fortunately, he had truly invested in the *Sales Yoga* approach and could grudgingly admit that his approach had been a little… brusque.

"Okay Scott, I see what you're getting at. I just wanted to do this as fast as possible and I guess I kind of steamrolled them. What do I do to fix it?"

"Mike, it seems to me that you've got two choices: You can abandon the system which makes them right for rebelling and not doing it, or you can fire them for not doing the system you told them to implement."

By the look on Mike's face, I was pretty sure neither of those options was attractive.

"That doesn't make sense, Scott. This was partially my fault for presenting this so badly. I know there's another option so what is it?"

"Okay Mike, I see I've made my point. So, how about this instead? How about coming back at it in a different way? Go back to your team and let them know you didn't roll out this system in the best of ways so you'd like to give it another shot.

"And, while you're at it, why not start it off with asking them about some of the things they dislike about selling in general. It would benefit you and your approach to know more about their experience."

"Okay, I could do that."

"And, based on their responses, take that new information and integrate it into the questions you ask them. For example, you would ask them what they don't like about selling and you'll probably get a whole list of things that frustrate or discourage them. From that list, you pick one or two things and ask them what they think would be a better way of going about it. Keep doing this until you hear enough to tie *Sales Yoga* into what they've shared."

Mike had a small smile on his face by the time I was done explaining.

"You're really asking me to do a coaching approach, aren't you?"

"Yes Mike, I am. You understand coaching. It's not about getting people to do the things you want them to, it's about having people talk themselves into making their own best choices. Just like *Sales Yoga* is about getting buyers to talk themselves into buying."

Mike went in to his next staff meeting and did just that. He asked questions, integrated the information and worked to develop a deeper understanding of his employees' needs. He learned about what they liked and disliked about selling and what he learned was very interesting. One thing he didn't anticipate hearing was the tremendous pressure his salespeople felt to solve the customers' problems.

"Scott, right there was my connection for *Sales Yoga*. The customer always believes themselves and only sometimes believes you. I took what I'd learned about the pressure to be problem-solvers and showed them how these techniques can help take much of the pressure off. I said,

"Our job is not to solve every problem. If we tried, we'd catch all the blame when things didn't go our clients' way. Our job is to get the customer to sell themselves on a potential solution. The customer will tell us what they need when we ask the right questions and often they'll also generate a couple of solutions. Since they thought of it and we just support and help clarify, they feel like it was a collaborative process both in the development of the solution, and the responsibility.'

"And that was that. They all said: 'Sign me up.'"

Mike had done a pretty bad job of presenting *Sales Yoga* the first time around. By using that heavy-handed Sales Boss approach, he managed to undermine and discredit the system at the same time he was presenting it. Through his willingness to ask for help, a self-awareness of his mistakes, Mike was able to ask for a second chance and his entire staff benefited.

What really solidified his employees' buy-in was a question Mike asked near the end of the meeting. He asked,

"What will happen when you start using this system?"

It was a simple enough question but, just like all provocative *Launching Questions*, it prompted them to use their imaginations and project into the future how client interactions would go now that they had this new information. Through that visualization, they began to generate enthusiasm for the *Sales Yoga* techniques through their anticipated success.

As they generated more stories, theories and scenarios, Mike kept asking more questions based on the information he'd gathered while learning what they disliked the most about selling.

"What will happen when you solve the problem, if the client was involved in the solving process?"

Rather than just supplying the answers, he helped them come up with their own.

People always believe themselves and only sometimes believe you.

When training or teaching, it can be so difficult to resist the temptation to supply all the answers. We've gone through school, workshops, trainings, staff meetings and have our own work experience as a reservoir of knowledge. When our staff is struggling, the impulse is to heap our wealth of knowledge upon them.

While this approach feels good for us, because it solidifies our stance as the expert in the room, it rarely does much good for the person on the receiving end of it. People are much more likely to retain, and invest in new information when they have a hand in the discovery process.

And, the discovery process isn't just spouting out an answer. It involves discussion, debate, pros and cons, imagination, and consideration. The more someone is permitted the chance to explore new information the more likely they are to integrate it, and at a much faster rate. It benefits us as leaders to resist the momentary temptation of depositing answers in someone's lap when the discussion process, laden with questions and visualization, will benefit both of you much more.

Action Plan for Chapter 25

"Change and growth take place when a person dares to become involved with experimenting with his own life." – Herbert Otto

Consider a training that's coming up soon, something in which you will have a hand in delivering information. If you've been planning a presentation, take some time to consider how you might transform your lecture into a conversation. The conversation doesn't have to be directly with you. You can break a large group up into smaller ones and have them discuss amongst themselves.

Here's how a discussion activity might go:

---

1. Break everyone up in small groups of no more than eight.
2. Have them all sit facing one another.
3. Have each group select a spokesperson.
4. Provide each group with a provocative question, such as, "How can we be more collaborative with our customers?"
5. Give them 10-15 minutes to generate a discussion.
6. Walk around the room and make sure the conversations are on track.
7. Provide additional questions to deepen the discussion if needed.
8. Give a two-minute wrap-up warning.
9. Call everyone back to the larger group and ask the spokespeople to briefly report what his or her group discussed and learned.
10. Keep track of what is shared and identify some points to clarify
11. Ask your integrative questions to the large group and see who responds.
12. Encourage cross-group participation at that point.

This approach can be used in your personal life as well. If you are looking to add a new routine, rule or tradition to your family or friends, take the time to present your ideas in the form of a question and ask for lots of feedback. Focus on helping them imagine the benefits *to them*, if they were to implement your suggestion. Make sure to equally honor any disagreement and be prepared to consider alternatives if someone offers a better suggestion.

Chapter 26:
The Power of Referrals

"If you work just for money, you'll never make it. But if you love what you are doing, and always put the customer first, success will be yours."

– McDonalds founder Ray Kroc

In one of my teleclasses a few years back, I assigned some homework that really ticked someone off. That someone was Jackie, a 30-something sales executive from Delaware. I couldn't see the level of Jackie's anger while I was teaching the Power of Referral techniques. The homework assignment was to simply add the word "help" to their referral request and for some reason, Jackie was not pleased and she later told me,

"There I was, sitting on the other end of that phone, having paid all that money to work with you and all I get is one, measly little word! I was so mad."

She left the teleclass vowing to never complete the homework. We were going to meet again in a week's time to discuss the homework. But, Jackie planned to continue on with her tried and true techniques for the global insurance firm she worked for.

So she continued working on referrals for the rest of the week and was getting nowhere fast.

"In the back of my mind was this stupid homework assignment you gave us to just add the word 'help' to our request for referrals. The more I did it my way, the more frustrated I got. So finally I decided I had nothing to lose and gave it a shot."

Jackie made her next phone call and changed nothing but adding the word "help" into her request and immediately got two referrals.

"To be honest, I thought it was a fluke. I'd made enough phone calls that one of them finally had to work. But, after another hour's worth of calls with nothing but that little change got me another 20 referrals, I had to admit it wasn't a fluke."

And, as they say in the MasterCard commercials, it was priceless.

"Scott," she told me. "That one word: help, was priceless. I couldn't believe the immediate effect it had on the way people were responding to my request. It changed the dynamic and I was no longer just a salesperson. I was just one human being asking another human being for help. I really think the reason it worked was because I genuinely wanted the help. It was an authentic request and people could sense that when I was willing to put the word to the feeling."

The beauty is you don't even have to believe it's going to work. Just genuinely ask for help and the help will come. In *Sales Yoga*, being genuine and authentic is how you build your trusting relationships with the people around you. For Jackie, the Power of Referrals breathed new life into her approach in a way nothing else could.

Yoga is all about breath, called Ujjayi breath or "the ocean breath." If you focus on nothing else, your breath is your primary venture and your goal is a deeper, smoother, more rhythmic and authentic breath. This is going to be true of your interactions with others, as well, using *Sales Yoga*. The deeper your understanding, the smoother your conversations, the more rhythmic and authentic the interactions, the more successful your ventures are going to be.

Buyers are sick of slick salespeople. They can tell when they're being manipulated, coerced and deceived. We bear the burden of reputation for all the salespeople before us and our task to change the face of our industry is an important one. The simple fact is people don't really have to rely on us as much as they used to. Internet marketing and sales is becoming more and more powerful.

Our greatest asset is human interaction, something our customers are screaming for, and we can approach them with new and authentic intent. We can be that "real person" on the other end of the line when they're "sick of talking to computers." But, we have to be better than the computers!

When it comes to referrals, the old school sales model is based on something called the Law of 250 developed by Joe Gerard, in *How to Sell Anything to Anybody*. It was based on the premise that everyone knows between 250 - 500+ people. He based this premise on the average number of people in attendance at weddings and funerals in their working years.

Today that is no longer the case because we are the generation of Facebook and Twitter. Social media has expanded our connection base beyond that 250 and well into the 500+ range. The Power of Referrals is about consistently asking everyone for help. The two key words in here are:

1) Everyone
2) Help

"Everyone" now means something much different than it did with the Law of 250. It is now the *Law of Expansive Contacts* because we are able to connect with people in ways we never have before. That's why we have to change the way we talk to these contacts. It's not just previous clients or people at a business convention anymore. It's everywhere we go and everyone we meet. It is now appropriate to ask anyone for help.

Now asking for help is about the human instinct for altruism. We see this every day with someone opening a door, volunteering in their community or giving to a charity. People help each other, even when they don't have to and that is the human instinct we want to work with. Now, like Jackie, we need to be genuine and authentic in our request.

We can even take this one step further and talk about something I call *Enrolling Language*. This is about choosing the right wording, based on the current culture that helps the other person share your need to help rather than make them feel manipulated or demanded of. You're tapping in to their human nature.

Sociolinguistic research tells us that people typically have three responses to language or words: positive, negative or neutral. And, as you can imagine, people typically respond in a positive way to the word "help." There are other key words that we should use in place of the typically negative word "referral." Because of this word's chronic misuse in the sales world, people tend to respond with, "I don't know anyone" or "let me think about it," when asked for one. Here are some enrolling words that get a better response:

- Support – "I need some *support*."
- Assistance – I could use your *assistance*.
- Connect – I'm looking to *connect* with other conscientious leaders like you.
- Meet – I'm hoping to *meet* the director of the department to discuss some mutual interests.
- Advice – I'd value your *advice*.
- Suggestion – Your *suggestions* would be very helpful.
- Recommendation – I'm told you give great *recommendations*.

And, when we use these words in a question, we want to wrap them in a *Launching Question*, rather than a *Locking Question* as salespeople will typically do. For example:

Locking Questions:

"Do you know anyone that would be interested?"
"Do you know anyone I could talk to?"
"Do you have any recommendations?"

Launching Questions:

"Who might be interested in these opportunities?"
"Who do you suggest I speak with?"
"Who do you recommend I talk to?"

Here are some questions to ask yourself to gauge how well you are leveraging the *Law of Expansive Contacts*:

- How often are you receiving referrals?
- What percentage of people do you actually ask for referrals?
- Why do you believe that you don't ask everyone for referrals?
- How will this actually help them as you help yourself in asking for referrals?

If it's less than 100%, it's time to seize this tremendous opportunity to put the Power of Referrals to work for you and your company.

Action Plan for Chapter 26

"The future is completely open, and we are writing it from moment to moment." – Pema Chodron

One of the many beautiful things about *Launching Questions* is they open a mutually beneficial future that we verbally write together, moment by moment.

Using *Launching Questions* allows people to access deeper memories and explore their options, rather than provide the surface yes or no answer that *Locking Questions* elicit. You can do this at the end of any conversation in this four-step process:

---

1. **Permission**: Because your original conversation wasn't about referrals.
2. **Why**: Help people understand your motives to take away any fear of what you are going to do with the requested information.
3. **Who:** Who are you looking to connect with? This is your guidance to them.
4. **Launch**: Your *Launching Question* to ask for help.

Here's what that conversation might sound like:

1. **Permission:** "Hey Mike, thanks for taking the time to talk with me. I appreciate all that information. (Wait for acknowledgement) May I ask for your help on a different matter?"
2. **Why:** "Part of my job is networking and I am responsible for connecting with other people that I can be of service to. That's why I'd like your help."
3. **Who:** "I'm looking to connect with people who are decision makers and buyers just like you in the widget industry (you can mention a couple of industries, two or three types, maximum)."
4. **Launch:** "Who do you suggest I speak with?"

Tips:

- Set up a follow up date if the person being asked needs to check or reflect.
- Keep your voice low toned and slow paced to be felt as safe and engaging.
- Don't judge a potential referral source by their cover; people may surprise you with who they know.

Section 4:
Action Plan and Summary

"Let us then be up and doing."

– Longfellow

Chapter 27:
What's Next? Create Your Sales Yogi Destiny

"In every childhood, there is a moment when a door opens and lets the future in."

– author Graham Greene

One of the purposes of this book is to offer collaborative approaches for selling to counteract the bad rap salespeople have earned over the years.

I know it may sound grandiose, but I believe that sales can be and should be one of the most respected professions across the globe. My hope is that this book opens doors to more ethical, effective ways of selling that lead to a more positive future for you and everyone you deal with.

As discussed, one of our priorities is to replace the old-fashioned "Always Be Closing" approach with the *Sales Yoga* "Always Be Collaborating" approach.

Glengarry Glen Ross	***Sales Yoga***
• A = Always	• A = Always
• B = Be	• B = Be
• C = Closing	• C = *Collaborating*

This book has introduced how to create *Launching Questions* that help you get to know your clients' true needs (even the ones they don't know about) so you can offer innovative solutions that lead to mutually prosperous relationships.

This book has also shared a variety of ways to integrate the practice of yoga into your practice of sales. Just as the Tree Pose can help us learn to stand tall and stand our ground, the Bridge Pose can help us understand that *Sales Yoga* is a "bridge" between being a quality salesperson...and a quality human being.

Create a Personalized Action Plan

"There's only one corner of the universe you can be sure of improving, and that's your own self." – Aldous Huxley

Remember earlier in the book when we talked about only being able to remember seven bits of information in our working memory?

We have covered a lot of information in this book—27 chapters worth of insights, examples, to-do's, not-to-do's and recommendations—and there's no way you can keep all of this top of mind when dealing with your buyers.

So, here's what I recommend.

Take 10 minutes to review the book. Scan through the pages and pull out the seven ideas or action items that were *most* timely or relevant for you.

Write them out—or type them out—using the format on the next page. Then, post it where you can see your *Sales Yoga* Best of the Best throughout the day so you keep your aha's in-sight, in-mind.

Then, do one more thing. I guess you can tell I like quotes. To me, they're a way to offer distilled pearls of wisdom in a provocative sentence or two. Go back through the book and pull out the quotes that stopped you in your mental tracks and got your attention. Select seven that would keep you inspired and that would keep you clear about who you want to be and how you want to show up.

As you move forward in the weeks, months and years ahead, promise yourself you'll review the book on the first Monday of every quarter.

You may see an insight that didn't resonate with you before but now it's perfect for a challenging situation you're dealing with. You may see a quote as if for the first time that has fresh meaning for you.

Want another way to increase the tangible impact this book has on you and your sales team? Buy a copy for every one of your employees. Announce that you'll be working your way through the book, together, one chapter per meeting.

Remember my suggestion to rotate the chair/host of your weekly sales meeting to give employees a chance to develop their leadership skills? It's not too late to do something similar with this book. Agree to discuss a chapter at each meeting and have a different employee facilitate the discussion so you and your team members are learning from each other how best to put these ideas into action.

Through our collective efforts, we can change the face of selling, one salesperson, one customer, and one conversation at a time. Imagine how much better it will be to sell in a world where all salespeople are highly revered instead of buyers running scared.

Action Plan for Chapter 27

"Destiny is not a matter of chance, it is a matter of choice; it is not a thing to be waited for, it is a thing to be achieved." – *William Jennings Bryan*

My Top Seven Aha's and Best Practices That I Want to Keep In-Sight, In-Mind Are:

1.

2.

3.

4.

5.

6.

7.

My Favorite Quotes About Being a Sales Yogi Are:

1.

2.

3.

4.

5.

6.

7.

Sales Yoga ...

by Scott Wintrip

About the Author ...
Scott Wintrip

What happens when you combine a brilliant consultant, an engaging speaker, a renowned executive coach...and the originator of an evolutionary sales process?

You get Scott Wintrip of the Wintrip Consulting Group (WCG).

Since 1999, Scott has worked with such clients as Proctor & Gamble, Boeing, Wells Fargo, American Red Cross, Discover Financial, Kohl's, Randstad, AFLAC, and MAKO Surgical. He has delivered presentations throughout Europe, Asia, South America, the U.S. and Australia.

Scott has served as an adjunct professional at St. Petersburg College and has been credentialed as a Professional Certified Coach by the International Coach Federation. During the past decade he was named to *Recruiter Magazine's* Top 40 Under 40, a list of the most powerful and influential executives under 40 years of age, and was a recipient of the prestigious Golden Rule Award.

In 2011-13, Scott was named to The Staffing 100, a list of the 100 most influential people serving the staffing industry. He was also inducted into the Million Dollar Consultant Hall of Fame, in recognition for being an exemplar in the consulting profession.

Scott admits his SSOP (Sales Standard Operating Procedure) used to be the "close at any costs" mentality he was taught. Then, he discovered yoga.

His family, clients and co-workers all noticed his renewed energy and more peaceful outlook and approach. They asked, "What happened?!" When he told them about the amazing transformation yoga had set into motion, they told him, "You should write a book about this. Other people could benefit from what you've learned." *Sales Yoga* is the result. Now, thousands have discovered the many positive rewards of integrating the timeless principles of yoga into their professional and personal interactions.

Want to Work
with Scott Wintrip?

You don't have to be a salesperson to benefit from Scott Wintrip's keynotes, consulting and advisory services, coaching, and workshops.

Face it...we'll all in sales. Anytime we have an idea, product, service or request that we want approved, bought or recommended—that involves selling.

As you've discovered through the varied examples in this book, you can use *Sales Yoga* approaches at work with clients and co-workers *and* at home with your kids. The many success stories throughout this book show that everyone benefits when you use *Sales Yoga* because these techniques help you treat people with the respect they want, need and deserve, which motivates them to respond in kind.

Want Scott to speak at your convention?

Please contact him at Scott@ScottWintrip.com or visit WintripConsultingGroup.com. Scott consistently receives raves from meeting planners who praise his ability to deliver real-world takeaways that keep their audiences engaged, from start to finish. Want Scott to customize a consulting program for your group? Contact him at Scott@ScottWintrip.com.

Scott is renowned for his ability to help his clients produce dramatic bottom-line results that meet and exceed their sales goals. In fact, Tracy R. Rettie, CAE, Assistant Vice President at ASA says, *"I have been working with you for over twelve years and you are one of the most reliable, responsive and supportive consultants that I work with. And believe me, I work with many!"*

When you're ready to transform how you or your organization sells, contact Scott and learn how to become a Sales Yogi.

www.ingramcontent.com/pod-product-compliance
Lightning Source LLC
Chambersburg PA
CBHW051449170526
45166CB00001B/181